A CUP OF COMFORT
for
Couples

Stories that celebrate
what it means to be in
Love

Edited by Colleen Sell

A adams media
Avon, Massachusetts

For Geronimo: the love of my midlife . . . and the rest of my life

A *Cup of Comfort*® is a registered trademark of F+W Media, Inc.

Published by
Adams Media, a division of F+W Media, Inc.
57 Littlefield Street, Avon, MA 02322 U.S.A.
www.adamsmedia.com and *www.cupofcomfort.com*

ISBN 10: 1-4405-0200-5
ISBN 13: 978-1-4405-0200-2
eISBN 10: 1-4405-0908-5
eISBN 13: 978-1-4405-0908-7

Printed in the United States of America.

10 9 8 7 6 5 4 3 2 1

Library of Congress Cataloging-in-Publication Data
is available from the publisher.

This publication is designed to provide accurate and authoritative information with regard to the subject matter covered. It is sold with the
understanding that the publisher is not engaged in rendering legal,
accounting, or other professional advice. If legal advice or other expert
assistance is required, the services of a competent professional person
should be sought.

—From a *Declaration of Principles* jointly adopted by
a Committee of the American Bar Association and
a Committee of Publishers and Associations

Many of the designations used by manufacturers and sellers to distin-
guish their products are claimed as trademarks. Where those designations appear in this book and Adams Media was aware of a trademark
claim, the designations have been printed with initial capital letters.

This book is available at quantity discounts for bulk purchases.
For information, please call 1-800-289-0963.

Contents

Acknowledgments

All books are collaborative creations, but none so much as an anthology. As the anthologist of this superb collection of true stories of true love, then, I have many people to thank:

Most gratefully, the authors of the forty-eight terrific stories that grace these pages,

As well as authors of the other 2,000-plus stories submitted for this book;

The gifted and generous folks at Adams Media— especially my chief collaborator, Meredith O'Hayre; *Cup of Comfort*® creator, Paula Munier; Karen Cooper, publisher; Casey Ebert, copy chief; and Beth Gissinger, publicist;

My parents, Albert and Jeannie Sell, for sixty years of demonstrating that love really is a many-splendored thing;

And with all my heart, my lover, best friend, favorite dance partner, life partner, and husband—Nik.

Introduction

*"And what do all the great words come to in the
end, but that?—I love you—I am at rest with you—I
have come home."*

—*Dorothy L. Sayers*

What is the secret to a successful marriage or
romantic partnership? How do you find true
love—and stay in love? Is love enough to weather
life's storms, petty grievances, and foolish mistakes?
Can you give your all to love without giving up your
self? Does a relationship that "works" take work, or
does it come naturally, easily? Do couples who live
happily ever after know something or have something or do something that couples whose relationships falter or fail don't?

Those are the questions most of us ask at one time in our lives—and that some of us ask repeatedly throughout our lives. Because deep in our hearts that's what most of us want: to love and to be loved by that one special someone.

So those are the questions we posed when we cast the net for true stories about couples who were truly, madly, deeply in love . . . or perhaps simply comfortable and content with and committed to one another. We asked couples to show us what true love, a good relationship, and a happy marriage look and feel like—to show us what makes them tick, together. So they did. From the more than 2,000 true stories of true love we received, we gathered the best into this book.

A Cup of Comfort® for Couples gives you an inside look into the hearts and lives of forty-eight couples. I hope their stories will delight, inspire, and move you.

—Colleen Sell

Supersized Love

My heart skipped three beats when the phone rang and I saw Ray's name on caller ID. Would it be a concert at Washington Park? A starlit run in Portland's west hills? A bike ride out to the beach at Sauvie Island?

"Samantha?" His deep, warm voice raised goose bumps on my arms.

"I know this is late notice, but are you free tonight?"

It was late notice, but I wanted to see him.

When I met Ray at a summer singles'–club dance, his hazel eyes, crooked smile, and lean but muscular physique immediately caught my attention. He invited me to hike the Eagle Creek Trail in the Columbia Gorge for our first date, and I shivered with excitement. Tickets to a Bruce Springsteen concert prompted a perfect second date. What would he

3

entice me with this time? Every woman knows third dates can often be turning points in relationships.

"How about meeting me at Costco for dinner?" Ray asked with the same lilt in his voice I'd have expected if he were inviting me to dine at the posh Harborside on the Willamette River.

I sank into a chair, unable for a moment to say anything. Was he kidding?

"I need to pick up some things for a catering job. They have a great Polish dog. Pizza or chicken wraps if you'd like that better."

He wasn't kidding. I have a Costco card and appreciate the prices, the quality, and the easy return policy as much as anyone. But a big cement warehouse with everything in supersize for a third date? Where were the candles? The music? Would he reach across a display of Sonicare toothbrushes to take my hand?

"Sure. I'll meet you there," I said, focusing on those hazel eyes and ignoring a fluttering of disappointment in my chest.

"Six-thirty?"

"That works," I agreed.

We met at the cavernous entrance, Ray already with a green flat cart in tow. He looked good, his yellow golf shirt setting off a nice tan. We flashed our cards at the attendant, ID pictures visible, and I trailed Ray and the cart as he walked purposefully to the back of the store, the aroma of fresh muffins wafting toward us.

"Wow," I gasped at all the six packs and twelve packs of juices and soft drinks he swung onto the cart.

"Big party," he said, moving to the section of paper products for plates and cups, then the frozen food section for meatballs and shrimp. Fresh fruit next: blueberries, strawberries, cantaloupe, watermelons, bananas.

I touched his shoulder. "Those are going to be beautiful fruit trays."

"Hope so."

Ray took good care of his customers. I sensed he would take good care of me as well. Shopping with him, I felt a surprising intimacy as I watched him do his thing as the owner of a small restaurant.

We continued to date, mixing Costco runs with movies, theater, fall hikes, and winter sports. I met his adult children; he met my teenagers. Then one day at Costco, when we'd been dating five months, he grabbed a regular, red-handled shopping cart, not a green flat cart. "I need to get a few things for my apartment," he said and proceeded to load a box of bottled water, a two-loaf pack of whole-grain bread, eggs, and a jar of peanut butter.

When we reached the frozen food section, he held up a bag of chicken burritos. "Your kids like these?" he asked.

"How nice. They'd love them."

He tossed them in the cart.

We stopped next at the tables of fruit. "Like cantaloupe?" he asked, holding up a net with three melons. "I could keep one at my place and you could take two home."

My stomach flip-flopped. What was going on? He was shopping for *us*.

He pushed the cart to the center of the store where a dozen tables were piled high with clothes, rummaged through a stack of golf shirts, and came up with a green one and a white one. "Which do you think?" he asked, holding them up.

"Either one," I assured him. He'd look terrific in both.

He tossed them in the cart and then moved to a table of women's sweaters. "Like any of these?" he asked.

I went weak-kneed, now certain of the shift in our relationship. This was no business run. He was loading a cart with his and her things.

The red turtleneck I picked up felt as soft as a kitten's fur against my cheek.

"I like you in red. You want it?" Ray nodded toward the cart.

I'd never considered Costco a place to buy clothes. I was learning so much this trip I could hardly breathe. With Christmas approaching, the red sweater would be fun, especially if I were wearing it to holiday celebrations with Ray. We were definitely an item.

Christmas came, then New Year's, then Valentine's. Ray and I spent as much time together as possible. My kids adored him and so did I.

"You think you'll get married?" a girlfriend at the school where I taught asked.

I shrugged. My first marriage had been a dismal, gut-wrenching experience, and I wasn't eager to try that again. Nor had Ray dropped to one knee and proposed. I was fine with the status quo.

At least I thought I was. Recently, though, everywhere I went I noticed diamond earrings, diamond necklaces, diamond rings. I wasn't ready to pick up a copy of *Modern Bride*, but something was going on.

Ray did not appear to share my obsession. When I shopped with him for his mom's birthday gift, he didn't even slow down as we passed the Zales, not to mention Tiffany.

That night we headed off to Costco for some laundry detergent, bathroom supplies, and a Polish dog. We flashed our cards as usual, but for once Ray didn't grab a cart. Assuming he'd forgotten, I turned back to get one. Gently but firmly he took my arm. In seconds he'd propelled me to the jewelry case. "See anything you like?" he asked.

A necklace for my June birthday? No, too early. I suddenly felt dizzy.

"I kind of like that one." He pointed to a perfect solitaire diamond set in a platinum band.

My mouth went dry.

"Do you want to look at it?"

I nodded.

He strode off and returned within seconds with a red-vested clerk who unlocked the case for us.

"That one." Ray pointed to the solitaire.

The clerk handed it to him.

"Want to try it on?" Ray threw me his fabulous crooked smile.

"Rings never fit me. I have huge knuckles like my dad." My voice trembled as I gazed at the ring he held out to me.

Ray steadied my left hand and slipped it on.

I stared at it. How could it fit so perfectly? And be so beautiful? Even in the fluorescent lighting of Costco, it sparkled like a meteor shower.

"What do you think?" Ray asked.

I answered with a kiss. Yes, right there in Costco. I could easily imagine our future. The wedding wouldn't be there, of course, but perhaps for our first anniversary Ray would say, "Want to go to Costco?"

And I wouldn't be able to think of anything more romantic than sitting across from him at a long, stainless steel table, eating a Polish dog and celebrating our supersized love.

—*Samantha Ducloux Waltz*

The Secret of Rugged Terrain

My baby's newborn squall pulled me from a deep sleep. I rubbed my eyes, pushed the covers back, and rolled from the comfort of our bed. Wake-up calls were so much easier a few years and several babies ago. We had five boys, and there were fifteen years between the oldest and youngest.

I bent over the bassinette and lifted my tiny son. Isaiah stopped crying; must've found the off switch.

"Is it morning already?" my husband, Lonny, asked from under our covers.

"It is now," I said.

Lonny sat up in bed, fluffed my pillow, and patted the mattress next to him. "Come here, you two," he said.

I handed him the swaddled newborn and curled in beside them. Isaiah settled into Lonny's chest. Lonny pulled the baby close, then tipped his own head and closed his eyes.

I admired their faces. The contrast was striking. Isaiah with his fresh, pink newborn skin. Unblemished. Dewey. Smooth. Lonny's complexion was tanned and rough. Lined. Like rugged terrain.

I kissed Lonny on the forehead and closed my eyes, too. As I huddled into the sweet warmth of my husband and son, I remembered back, long ago, when our marriage had been new and fresh—like the flesh of a newborn babe.

"Do you think this will last, Shawnelle? Being so happy?" Lonny asked.

We'd been married two weeks and were wrapped together in a deep, round futon chair. Our first apartment didn't have air conditioning, but we sat close anyway.

I took a bite of Lonny's cheese pizza. "Sure," I said. "Why shouldn't it?"

"Just seems too good to be true," he said.

I tousled his too-long hair. "Of course it will last."

But life came at us hard and fast. Lonny worked to finish college. I went to work for an elementary school near campus while he finished his degree. Then Lonny graduated, and we moved to mid-Michigan. New jobs. New community. I went back to school. A barrage of changes rushed at us, and we didn't know how to manage the stress together. We handled our own stuff in our own ways, and by the time we pulled that top-tier wedding cake from the freezer to celebrate our first anniversary, our marriage had grown chilly, too. We'd started to pick at one another, noticing the shortcomings and looking past the good things.

One day Lonny came home from work. Late. He'd missed dinner and been too busy to call. He kicked off his shoes, tossed his briefcase to the floor, padded to the dining room, and pecked me on the cheek.

"Sorry," he said. "Tough day. How was yours?"

"Long," I said. "Will you please put your shoes in the closet? I've picked them up a dozen times this week."

"Sure, after I grab something to eat," he said.

First he was late. Then the shoes. "How about now?" I said.

"How about later?" he said.

"How about I toss them on the lawn?"

"How about you finish the trim in the living room? Geesh, Shawnelle, I can't believe you painted the room and left the trim undone. Can't you finish what you start?"

He plunked down his plate on the table, and we ate in silence. I wished we could talk, but I couldn't guarantee that my words would be kind. I wanted them to be, but all I could think about were those darned shoes.

Such was our life. We weren't unhappy. But we weren't happy, either. We moved through life and time. Bought a house. Had a baby. There were good times, too, and neither of us wanted to bail. But we bickered constantly, and we were keenly aware of and quick to point out one another's shortcomings. We went on like this for a while—drawing out the flaws and glossing over the good stuff.

We'd been married a couple of years when I woke one morning, plodded to the bathroom, and perched on the side of the tub. It had been a long, sleepless night. The baby had a marathon earache and hadn't rested. I was still taking classes and had a test that afternoon. Lonny had worked late . . . again. I hadn't studied. The cupboards rivaled Mother Hubbard's. And the laundry was piled high.

I twisted the hot-water knob and rested my head in my lap while the water charged into the tub. When I lifted my head, I saw them. The socks. The dirty, grungy, left-on-the-floor athletic socks. And they weren't alone. There were also jeans, a T-shirt, and underwear. My pulse quickened.

"Lonny," I called. I hoped my agitation would stretch to the bedroom. "You left a pile of dirty laundry on the bathroom floor for me to pick up! How many times do I have to ask you?" My tone was sharp as glass as I poked at the lump of clothes with my bare toe. "I have so much to do today."

There was no response from the bedroom.

I grabbed the clothes and stalked down the hall. I pulled open the closet door and flipped the lid on the hamper that stood inside. As I pushed the clothes deep into the hamper, a white slip of paper wafted from the wicker and settled at my feet. I bent to pick it up.

It was a grocery receipt, from Lonny's jean pocket. My eyes roved over the faint purple print. Milk. Eggs. Bread. Lonny had worked late and done the shopping afterward—so I didn't have to.

Suddenly, the socks didn't seem like such a big deal.

I pushed the closet door shut and walked to the bedroom. I pulled back the covers on the bed and slid in beside my husband.

"Lonny," I said. "Wake up. We need to talk."

"What's up?" he murmured.

"I need to tell you that I'm sorry. I'm sorry for looking at the socks instead of your heart. Will you forgive me?"

"What are you talking about?" he asked. He sat up and squinted.

"I don't always see the good man you are. I fuss over small things. I'm sorry. And I love you."

"I love you, too. And you're right. We do need to focus on the good in each other." Lonny pulled me close. "We have a lot of work to do. But let's start in an hour or so." Then he gave me a gentle push. "Now, go away and let me sleep for a few more minutes. And look in the cupboard. Peanut butter Captain Crunch. Your favorite."

Lonny was right. We did have a lot of work to do. But we rolled up our sleeves and pushed ahead. We'd found our secret. We'd seen our need to look at one another's overall character—rather than the flaws.

That day was eighteen years ago. The years have blown by. We've learned to pull together. It didn't come easy. We've had some tough times. But the reward has been sweet.

I listened for Isaiah's soft, even breath. When I knew that he was sleeping, I got up, lifted him, and returned him to the bassinette. Then I snuggled in beside Lonny. He wrapped his arms around me. The way he has for a very long time.

Our marriage isn't newborn. It's not unblemished or fresh. It hasn't always been smooth. But I'm glad. I wouldn't want a newborn marriage again.

I'm happy for where we are.

I'm happy for where we've been.

There's a lot of love along that rugged terrain.

—*Shawnelle Eliasen*

First Love

"Time for our walk," he says. "Tide clock shows we've two hours before the beach disappears."

The morning sun crawls across our faces as we follow our black Lab through a gate of Inukchuks and across the meadow to a vine-covered shelter. My husband calls this hideaway our "Counting Room," a place to count our blessings. Blue herons, looking up from their breakfast of bass, stretch their necks in curiosity, then ignore two old folks.

Submerged in tranquility, we sit a while before wending our way through the woods and down to the shore. Whitecaps, as if in a hurry, thunder against the rocks and sand below the bluff, reminding me how quickly time has moved the years of our lives.

I look upon the face of the handsome man beside me and remember those years. Still riding around town on my bike and helping out at Ben's, my dad's lunchroom, I was just fifteen when I first met Bud. It was at a teen dance in town. He was older—eighteen—and had his girlfriend with him. But we walked home together that night, holding hands like two souls fulfilling a destiny.

Today, on his tired face I see all his eyes have seen. And much more. The wrinkles tell their stories: Stories of a crew-cut teenager who once considered becoming a priest but instead joined the Navy. Stories of a cocky, conceited young Navy pilot who always wore a Miraculous Medal while flying off Canada's last aircraft carrier.

"Glory days," he tells anyone who will listen. "Taking off and landing on Bonnie's seven-hundred-foot runway was pure heaven. After the adrenaline rush, the calmness was incredible."

We two became letter lovers. For years we shared stories of my studies and his days on the high seas. At first we wrote every Sunday afternoon. Then letters arrived daily. Sometimes his came in blue, tissue air letters posted at sea, other times stuffed into colorful envelopes with foreign postage. Jottings became journals. We helped one another through days of hard work—and nights of loneliness. Love evolved from deep friendship into true caring.

I see, too, on his face the story of a twenty-something lad proposing to a nineteen-year-old student nurse in a tiny chapel of St. Patrick's church. And the story of a honeymoon in an old 1954 Buick. I see a husband who cradled me in his arms and cried with me when our first-born baby died. And the enraptured awe upon that same face when he held each of our three healthy babies.

Upon his weathered face I see story lines of a lonely husband and father, who, after observing other nationalities with families in tow, wrote home asking his young family to pack up and join him on his "unaccompanied tour of duty" in a faraway land.

In Palestine, we lived a life that some would consider dangerous (a military coup and a plane hijacking), but the United Nations protected us. And as long as it remained reasonably safe, we vowed to keep our family together—moving from a house on a hill in Tiberias, Israel, overlooking the Sea of Galilee to a high-rise apartment in Damascus, Syria, the oldest continuously inhabited city in the world.

At the end of those two years in the Middle East, I see a father driving along the coast of Turkey, telling his children stories of kings and queens and Roman soldiers as we all snuggled in our VW camper. I see us cooking octopus beside the Aegean Sea, swimming off the beaches of Dubrovnik, and camping outside the cities of Athens and Venice. I see him safely maneuvering his family of five through the mountains of Germany, Austria, and Switzerland and to ports in France and England before sailing home on the SS *France*.

Under his furrowed brow, I see a protector who scoffed at the parenting trend of the seventies and eighties that recommended tough love for teenagers navigating the emotional minefields of changing hormones. Plunging into parenting with compassion, we tried desperately to figure out how much leeway to give while not overwhelming with rules and regulations. Many mistakes were made. "The fragile years," we called them, and "the twisted storms of life." Passion, even our love for one another, was tested, relegated to the back burners.

"But no regrets," he says, carrying the past with dignity. "We've lived and loved. Traveled. Dined with the best—even royalty. Time to nest a while," he laughs.

Like a rural road map, tiny webs of sorrow crisscross his ruddy cheeks, showing signs of life's sad sagas: the deaths of his younger brothers, the casualties of carrier flying, and the early demise of close friends who shared his love of aviation. Even the loss of our time together while he was away in Canada's capital is forever imprinted on his weathered face, a face etched with grief lines from many lonely nights.

But I also see the laugh lines beneath my husband's heavy brows. Stories of a self-deprecating grandfather enjoying time with grandchildren: kayaking on the bay, reciting poetry, spinning the same old yarns (over and over again), and spoiling them with pancake breakfasts topped with ice cream and chocolate chips and anything else needed to sweeten their young lives.

As I follow his footsteps down through the woods, I notice his shoulders a bit stooped, his pace a tad slower, his stride a little shorter. Too much time spent felling dead trees and lugging firewood. In Bud's mind, he's still twenty. But I can understand the strength that brought him to today, the stubbornness that kept him going. Never faltering, he trusted in small, everyday acts of loving kindness that continue to glue our lives together.

This headstrong, often cantankerous curmudgeon, this one-time member of Parliament, is my confidante. My soul mate. The sensuous person whose simplest touch still tingles my marrow. The man who encouraged me to pursue my university dreams, proudly applauding as I marched to the podium at age fifty. This gray-bearded gentle man is the lover whose arms guide me safely through the gates of life. The same gates through which tears and laughter flow freely.

Somewhere along the way, romantic love evolved into a more mature love and, although different, in many ways a much deeper love. Nowadays, we communicate without talking, disagree without hurting, hug for no reason at all, and dance if we want to.

I lengthen my stride in the sand to step carefully into his large footprints. He takes my hand, and we embrace. Closer now, I see much more than an old man's face. I see a man who has allowed his heart to get in the way of living. A man who has a story of life, of our life, on his face.

I see my husband of fifty years. I see my first love. My last love. My forever love.

—*Phyllis Jardine*

This story was first published in *Canadian Messenger of the Sacred Heart* magazine, fall 2010.

Matchmaker

"She needs a mother." The volunteer inclined her head toward the squirming ball of fur cradled in my arms. "She's the last of a litter, you know. All the rest have been taken."

"You've lost your family," I whispered, gazing into the almond-shaped eyes of the white kitten. "You're all alone. I know how that feels."

As a familiar pain lanced my heart, I pulled the cat closer and marched to the front desk. "I want to adopt her. Now. I want to give her a home."

Nestled in her cardboard pet carrier, Snowball serenaded me with plaintive meows as I drove through what passed for rush hour traffic in Camden, Maine. For my part, I kept up a steady stream of chatter, gentling my voice until she grew quiet. "There's a nice screened porch. You'll like that. Oh, and we get all sorts of birds, at least in the summer months. I don't know about the winters. I'm from New York, you see. I only just moved here." I hesitated, unwilling to admit, even to a cat, that coming to Maine had been a spur-of-the moment decision made in desperation. And in grief.

When I turned onto Bay View Road, the calming blue expanse of the harbor came into view and I began to relax. "We're home," I said, pulling to a stop beside the hydrangea bushes that flanked the entrance of my shingled cottage.

Once inside, I opened the carrier. Although Snowball poked her head out the opening, she didn't venture further.

"Better the devil you know, right?" I asked with a nod. "Trouble is, you can't see you're in a cage until you leave it behind."

I scooped the kitten into my arms and held her trembling body close. "Come on, I want to show you something." I made my way slowly across the room toward a wall dominated by floor to ceiling windows. "See?" I asked, holding her up to the glass. "That's the ocean, honey. It's where fish come from. Tuna and salmon and cod. You'll try them all, don't worry. And you'll see seagulls, too."

She looked around, her eyes scanning the sky as her tail flicked against my arm. Then she jumped down to sit before the window, tail curled around her body and pink nose pressed to the glass.

"It didn't take you long to feel at home, did it?" My eyes skimmed the living room's rich wood tones and creamy white furniture. "I don't yet." But then, I had more than a new home to get used to.

I'd been in Maine six months, and it had taken me two weeks before that to clean out the house in New York. One-hundred-ninety-five days in all. Marking the time since I'd lost my daughter had become a sort of ritual, as though by counting the hours I hadn't shared with her, I was keeping faith with the past.

Purring loudly, Snowball rubbed her head on my leg. "Thank you, honey," I said through tears.

We made our way to the kitchen, where I opened a can of tuna. The cat attacked her dinner with gusto. A little later, she made use of the litter box I'd devised out of a disposable lasagna pan and some shredded newspaper. Then she hopped back into her carrier and curled up for the night.

The next morning as dawn pearled the sky I came to a decision. When I phoned the shelter hours later, the woman who answered was brusque.

"That information is confidential."

"I can't see why it would be," I shot back. "Look, I just want to find out who adopted the other cats in the litter."

"But why?" Her voice was spiced with annoyance.

"To make sure they're happy in their new homes. If not, I'm willing to take them."

"Why?" she pressed.

I drew a steadying breath. "To keep the litter together, to reunite the family."

I heard the sound of shuffling papers. "Well, one of the cats went to someone who's moved out of state. The other was adopted by Michael Quinn, the veterinarian who's restoring that white Federal across from the library. Michael serves on our board. I don't think he'd mind speaking with you."

"Come on, honey," I said, scooting Snowball into her carrier. "Let's go find your family."

The town of Camden hugs the mid-coast of Maine, much as it has for two centuries. The protected harbor that birthed a shipbuilding industry is now dotted with schooners, yachts, and kayaks. It's a civilized place where the tourists are well-mannered and the shops quaint. Picturesque houses line quiet streets that separate the sea from the mountains beyond.

I pulled into Michael Quinn's circular drive with some trepidation, regretting my impulse to bring Snowball.

Making my way toward a columned side porch, I saw a middle-aged man sitting at a wrought iron table. His thick black hair was flecked with gray and he wore wire-rimmed glasses, a white T-shirt, and worn jeans. "Good morning," I called out. After introducing myself, I explained why I'd come.

Fixing me with striking blue eyes, Michael cocked his head and asked, "You want my cat?"

"Well, no. Er, yes. I mean, I want to make sure you're happy with him."

"Are you from the shelter?"

"No," I said. "I adopted the last of the litter and—" I stopped, feeling like an idiot.

"And you want to reunite the family, if possible. If not, you just want to make sure the other cats are being cared for—right?"

"Yes, exactly," I said, relieved to be so easily understood.

A cool breeze ruffled the blond curls I'd never succeeded in taming, and as I pushed at them impatiently, I caught a flicker of interest on his face. When he stood up, the muscles beneath his shirt rippled and a voice in my mind reminded me that I was still a young woman.

"Well, come inside," he offered, gesturing toward the door. "But I warn you: I'm not giving up Louie."

"Louie?" I repeated, taking an awkward step forward. "You named him Louie?"

"For Louis Armstrong," he explained. "The cat loves jazz."

We stood together in the dimly lit foyer for a moment before a tuxedo black-and-white cat bounded down the stairs and came to rest at his owner's feet.

Bending down to scratch Louie's belly, Michael suggested, "Why don't you get yours?"

"Mine?"

He cocked his head. "I assume you brought him with you?"

"Her, actually," I corrected. "Snowball."

While the cats chased each other through the house, paws skidding on the polished wood floors and fur flying as they batted each other playfully, Michael and I shared a pot of coffee, then a bottle of wine, and finally a casual dinner. He told me of his divorce, and I found the words to describe the night I'd lost Lucy.

"We were on our way to the animal shelter. My husband had died a year before, and I'd been working all the hours God sent to make ends meet. And to forget. But I'd promised Lucy a white kitten for her seventh birthday, so I left work early that day to take her. She'd even picked out a name: Snowball."

My voice caught, but I made myself go on. "The truck came out of nowhere, plowed right into us. I was thrown clear and knocked out. When I woke up, flames were everywhere. I tried to get up but kept falling. So I crawled toward the car, screaming for Lucy. I managed to pull her free before it exploded. I felt her body shudder and held my breath, as though by refusing to live I could force her to."

My voice fell to a whisper. "I remember her first breath. The clear scream of greeting all mothers wait for. But her last breath, her last breath was as quiet as a sigh."

Michael listened until the words and the tears slowed to a trickle. "And afterward, you decided to move here?"

I nodded. "We'd always talked about living by the water. Lucy loved Maine."

"And you adopted the cat your daughter would have."

"I didn't intend to. Oh, I knew about the shelter here, but I'd avoided the place for months. I just couldn't . . . "

He nodded in understanding, and I swallowed hard.

"Yesterday, I found the courage to go there," I said. "Just to drop off some food."

My eyes strayed to where Snowball had fallen asleep on the edge of the couch, her head hanging over the side and her tail tucked between her front paws. "She was just so cute," I smiled at the memory.

"I had to pet her. Then hold her. Well, one thing led to another . . . "

He nodded. "It was the same with me and Louie. I had no intention of getting a cat. Of course, he had other ideas. Fixed me with those big eyes of his, and I was lost."

I shifted my gaze from the sleeping cats to his concerned face. It was a good face, I decided.

"You know," he continued in a matter-of-fact voice, we should get them together for play dates. That way, they won't forget each other, and we can get to know one another."

When I stiffened in response, he added hastily, "As friends. I mean, you're new to town, and I've lived here forever. I could show you around."

At the expectant look on his face, I nodded and the knot around my heart began to loosen.

Michael and I began spending time together, and our relationship grew so gradually, it's difficult to know when we crossed the line from friendship to love. We had a simple wedding ceremony on the summit of a mountain overlooking the harbor town I'd come to think of as home. Michael moved into my house, and the comforting routine of our marriage helped wear smooth the jagged memories of my life before. When we were blessed with a child, I searched the solemn eyes of our infant girl and found nothing of Lucy. A part of me died that day, but another part began to heal.

Our daughter, Sara, is now fifteen and has grand plans: she wants to be a veterinarian like her father. Michael is thrilled at the thought of sharing with Sara his practice and stewardship of the shelter we now run.

Our cat, Louie, still makes an effort to run around the house, but most evenings he lounges before the fire waiting for us to rub his belly. The years have been less kind to Snowball. Arthritic and nearly blind, she rarely ventures beyond the quilts I scatter about the floor in a pattern meant to catch the sun as it moves throughout the day. Although my heart aches at the thought of losing her, I know that when she passes, Lucy will be waiting for her.

When Snowball hears my voice, she purrs in greeting and waits to be picked up. I hold her close and whisper her name, one that anchors me to the life I had before and reminds me of how blessed I am to have found Michael. Snowball, my little matchmaker.

—*Ariella Golani*

My Other Husband

I have been happily married for twenty-nine years . . . to two men. Fortunately, they both occupy the same body, so I'm not in danger of being carted off to prison anytime soon.

Husband number one's name is Fred—a hard-working mechanical engineer, quiet, reserved, an honorable man. Intelligent and analytical, he's a no-nonsense kind of guy on whom I can depend no matter what kind of crisis comes along. I am a free spirit, usually led by emotions, not logic; my response to most serious problems is to laugh and let God worry about them. Fred's is to weigh out the circumstances and calculate an appropriate course of action.

We are two very different personalities. So when people I know meet Fred for the first time, they are usually surprised. "He's so . . . serious," they say.

I just smile because they don't know my "other" husband, Freddie.

I'll give you a for instance. You know how boring grocery shopping is? Not with Freddie. When he comes with me, this is usually how it goes:

We walk into the market and Freddie says, "I wanna push the cart!"

"Why?"

"I'm the man; I push the cart."

"Okay. Whatever."

And the adventure begins. I'm standing there trying to figure out which soup is the best buy, and when I go to put the chosen one into the cart, Freddie runs about six steps ahead. So I run to catch up, and he sprints about eight to ten steps farther on. Before long, I'm chasing him up and down the aisles, and we're laughing like fools, and people are beginning to stare.

Finally, stifling a giggle, I grab the vehicle away from him. "Okay, mister, you've lost your cart-pushing privileges! I'm pushing the cart from now on."

"Hmmph."

The minute I set my purse in the bask jumps on the front—effectively stalling stands.

"Get off the cart, Freddie."

"I wanna ride!"

"You're heavy. Get off!"

"You don't love me."

"Oh, for crying out loud. All right, but behave yourself."

I'm checking out the prices on the paper towels, and when I turn around, Freddie, now off the cart and about fifteen feet away, is in his Michael Jordan mode—making basket after basket with assorted brands of toilet paper. There are now approximately twenty packages of tissue in my basket.

Trying not to laugh, and thus to encourage him, I yell, "*Stop that!*"

People are gathering to watch.

Freddie, all innocence, asks, "What?"

I put all the toilet tissue back on the shelf and continue down the aisle. Freddie has disappeared, thank goodness. For the next five minutes, I finish my shopping in peace.

At the checkout counter, the clerk is ringing up my groceries when I stop her. "Hey, those aren't my ice cream bars."

"Uh, they were in your basket, ma'am."

"How did those four packages of Cheetos get in there?"

"Hmmm," she says with a lifted eyebrow. "You might want to ask him." She points at Freddie, who has suddenly appeared from out of nowhere, grin-
ing like a hyperactive four-year-old.

I look at him suspiciously. "Where have you been?"

"Just messin' around."

The clerk waves for my attention. "So will you be wanting this package of chicken feet?"

"*Freddie!*"

At this point, Freddie gives me his most lovable grin and in his best Bart Simpson voice says, "Ha ha! You love me!"

"No, I don't. You're a pain in the butt."

"Yes, you do!"

I sigh. "Okay. I do. But I don't have to like it."

By now, the clerk and the three people behind us in line are laughing out loud.

In the car as we drive home, Freddie goes into his bet-I-can-drive-you-crazy mode, grabbing my knee, tickling the back of my neck, rolling my window up and down.

"Quit it, Freddie!"

The response is, of course, an escalation of the behavior—until I give him The Look, and he settles down.

All is quiet for the next quarter mile, then suddenly he says, "Ha ha!"

I groan. "Ha ha, what?"

"Ha ha!" he repeats, tickled with himself. "You're married to me!"

So, you see, I have the best of what marriage can be. I have a husband who is a rock in every storm and a steadfast partner in a serious marriage. A husband who shows me he loves me with his hard work around the house and in his job, by handling our finances brilliantly, and displaying his affection frequently with a warm hug and a light kiss.

But I also get to live with a bona fide character, a best friend who constantly surprises me, who makes me laugh like nobody's business, and who honestly believes that affection is best shown by a well-timed, heartfelt wedgie.

Do I know what it means to be loved and in love? You betcha.

—Tina Wagner Mattern

Heart and Sole

W hen, at age twenty-five, I was about to marry my college sweetheart, there was no shortage of advice from my well-meaning Italian family on how to achieve and maintain marital bliss. Unfortunately, much of it was a bit too 1950ish for my taste and did not really fit marriage in the waning years of the twentieth century.

Have a warm supper on the table each night.

Yeah, right. My husband and I needed to pay for our expensive college degrees; we were up to our ears in student loans. Both of us would be working for years to come, and so we'd be fortunate to find the take-out food still warm by the time our plastic forks dug into it.

Bathe the kids and put them in clean clothes before he gets home.

When we finally did have kids, I was quite certain we'd be challenged enough trying to coordinate who would pick them up from daycare or baseball practice. The kids would be bathed no more than three times a week—if they were lucky.

Show him you appreciate him and are interested in him by redoing your hair and makeup at the end of the day.

Really? I'm barely up in time to do it right before I go to work.

Keep a tidy house, vacuum and dust frequently, and keep his closet and drawers filled with freshly laundered clothes.

Vacuum the house? Do his laundry? *Pffftthhh!* My vacuum would be buried under loads of laundry I had yet to fold—*my* laundry; surely Dan would do his own.

Don't go to bed angry.

This, I was sure, would be the most difficult bit of advice to follow. I don't easily let go of things I'm upset about. Neither does Dan, for that matter. And with all of the demands on our time, it was unlikely we would have much time to work things out before the lights were turned off for the night.

Frustrated with the seemingly impractical advice I had received, I turned to the two people who knew me best and who, coincidentally, had been married nearly fifty years: my grandparents. I figured they must have some good advice they would be willing to share—an advance on my inheritance perhaps, something I could pass on to my future children. So one day while sitting at their kitchen table as my grandmother cooked and my grandfather sat in "his" chair sipping a glass of wine, I asked the million-dollar question.

"Nonnie," I began.

"Yes, honey," she replied, opening the oven to baste the chicken.

"I'm looking for some advice."

"Advice about what, honey?"

The smells were tantalizing, and I inhaled deeply. "Everyone is telling me that for my marriage to work I need to do Dan's laundry, and keep the house clean, and bathe the kids, and get dolled up for him. That will be impossible. I'll have a job outside the home, too, and won't have the time to do all that. Besides, I expect Dan to do his share of the house-work and childcare, too. So what can I do to help our marriage last like yours and Grandpa's?"

Nonnie looked lovingly at Grandpa and said, "Touch him with your toes." Then she turned back to the oven to baste the chicken.

Touch him with my toes? That's as useless as all the other advice I've received, I thought. *Or was I missing something?*

"What do you mean, 'Touch him with my toes'?" I asked.

"Touch him with your toes. It's as simple as that."

"But, Nonnie, how is that supposed to help me have a long and happy marriage?"

She closed the oven door and turned to me. "Sweetie, you and Dan will have many arguments about the littlest things. And after some of those silly disagreements, you won't feel like sharing your bed with him. Be thankful that you have someone who loves you to share a bed with. Be thankful that you can touch him with your toes."

I had my doubts. How could touching toes ensure a lasting, happy marriage? Then again, who was I to question the validity of something that obviously worked for them? All I could do was ponder the possibility as I waited for Nonnie's delicious chicken and for my own marriage to begin.

A few months before their fifty-fifth wedding anniversary, Grandpa passed away. Since then, Nonnie has not spent one night in the bed they used to share. I'm quite certain that each night she imagines the feel of Grandpa's skin against the bottoms of her feet and the warmth that always radiated from his legs.

In the nearly two decades that my husband, Dan, and I have been married, more often than not I've used my toes in a not-so-gentle effort to encourage him to roll over and stop snoring. But there have been many times when, because pride and a stubborn Italian streak make it too difficult to apologize out loud, I gently touch his leg with my toes to say, "I'm sorry. Let's break down the barriers between us. Let's connect." And some nights, I place my feet mere inches from his leg just to feel his presence, grateful that I have someone—that I have Dan—to go through life with.

I am saddened by the certainty that someday I will no longer be able to touch Dan with my toes. But I am eternally grateful to my grandparents for their simple wisdom. For I am thankful to have someone who loves me to share a bed with, someone I can lie next to every night and touch with my toes. And when my children and my grandchildren are about to take their own nuptials, I will give them their "inheritance" as casually and as offhandedly as my grandparents gave mine to me: Touch toes.

—*Carolyn Huhn-Sullivan*

A Love Worth Waiting For

Once upon a time, more than three decades ago, to be precise, an Oregon writer met a Stockholm doctor in a San Francisco restaurant and they ended up touring the city together, talking and walking, walking and talking. The next weekend, he would be in Seattle, so she followed, and again they enjoyed many hours of talking and walking, walking and talking. As the woman drove south to her home in Oregon while he flew home to Sweden, she had the strange feeling of leaving her best friend.

When the two platonic friends had parted, they'd said they would not write. Yet, their letters crossed in the mail and continued across the continents, sharing careers, families, philosophy, their mutual love of nature. Surely they would never meet again, so the letters were honest and without guile.

Two years passed, and the Swedish doctor came to work in Seattle for a year. The man and woman met again, and began to fall in love. But he had a family to whom he was committed; she acknowledged that and honored his integrity. Once again, they reluctantly said farewell, and she went on to marry another.

Over the years, she would wonder about the man and ponder the what-ifs and if-onlys.

Nearly twenty years later, the woman had a dream. In the dream, the man stood in her kitchen with his wife. The wife—without sadness or anger—was turning over her husband to the woman. With a start, she awakened: *What could her dream mean? What on earth was happening in his life?*

At the very same time on the other side of the world, the man typed the woman's name into the Internet. Nothing. For months, he browsed the web, searching for the woman. Then, on this side of the globe, she typed in his name. Finally, they connected. His wife had died. She had divorced. Neither had forgotten the other.

Once more the letters and now e-mail crossed. Early one July morning, the woman got a call. She hadn't heard the man's voice in two decades. He was at a medical conference in Denver. Within three hours, she was on a plane, risking everything on a spontaneous surprise visit. In a convention room filled with three hundred people, she found him.

Twenty years spun back in time, and they were young again; nothing had changed.

Nothing but circumstances, that is.

In early November, the man flew the woman to his Sweden home for a two-week visit, which felt like a honeymoon.

They went shopping together to decorate the new home he had just built. They wound through the narrow, cobbled streets of Gamla Stan (Old Town Stockholm) and clambered four flights of a centuries-old building to meet his eighty-five-year-old mother, who greeted the woman with a hug. She met his three grown children, who thanked her for making their father so happy and presented her with a gift upon her departure. She met his best friends, and together they laughed like old companions.

They visited the cemetery on All Soul's Night, when families light candles and small lanterns on the graves. He spoke of the numbness, the pain, the daily walk through the woods to this green gravestone. At the wife's grave, the woman burst into tears. "I always wanted you but not at this price, never at this price!" she cried. The man and woman held each other, and came to understand that "for all things, there is a season."

Each day he brought her breakfast in bed. Once more, they talked and walked, and walked and talked, and the days were seamless, fluid, without effort. They cleaned, and they cooked, and they entertained. They listened to music and read aloud. They lit candles morning and evening against the cold November darkness. They traipsed the woods, and he showed her favorite places: the meadow the young parents had cleared late each spring for the children's Midsommar Festival, the swimming rock, the enchanted hollow tree where the kids once played.

They threw supplies into a duffel bag and climbed into his boat for the ninety-minute trip through the Stockholm Archipelago of 24,000 islands to his century-old cabin. The Baltic suddenly turned angry and wild, and she clung tightly to keep from being thrown from the banging boat while he steered them safely on. *I would trust my life to this man* she thought. *I already am.*

They hunkered in the one-room cabin while the wind pounded at the red plank door. As the corner fire warmed the room, they stripped off layers of clothing and loneliness. Candlelight reflected in the tiny windowpanes and one another's eyes in this wilderness on the edge of the world.

Each day they laughed and loved and learned more about the other. Each day they marveled that life just couldn't get better. And each day proved them joyously wrong.

Then, these two people who so savored living alone agreed they would live together. It was only as obvious as eating and breathing. "We have two wonderful places to live in, we love each other, and the rest is just details," the man said.

He introduced her to Tanzania, East Africa, where he had worked with HIV/AIDS for years. Unsatisfied to be simply a tourist, she asked the universe to steer her toward something important to do. The very same day she met a local woman busy stirring a pot of *ugali* in an outdoor kitchen, and the two talked. The woman met her new friend's sister, who invited her to see her village school.

Ever the adventurer, the woman climbed onto a crowded, rickety bus and rattled 10 miles south of Dar es Salaam to sprawling Mbagala, where they got out and walked through dusty lanes where tourists never go. "*Mzungo! Mzungo!*" small African boys shouted at the white woman. Babies looked her way and burst into tears, goats brayed, and eyes followed until they stopped at Fatuma's tiny home, where thirteen tots danced to the beat of a goatskin drum in a dingy room without toys or books.

The next day, the woman returned with school supplies and asked about the hand-high outline of cinderblocks in the yard.

"My dream is to build a real school," explained the middle-aged, divorced mother of four.

"Let me help," her new friend said.

When the couple married in Oregon and again in Sweden, they asked for school donations in lieu of gifts, and the cinderblocks grew higher with each visit. Fatuma named her new school Bibi Jann Day Care Center in honor of the woman (*bibi* being Kiswahili for grandmother). Eventually, the school grew through grade five and evolved to become Bibi Jann Children's Care Trust. AIDS orphans and the grandmothers raising them would come together under GRANDMA-2-GRANDMA to create goods to sell, and STUDENT-2-STUDENT began to educate the children, with sponsors worldwide for both programs. The journalist became a philanthropist/ social worker/fundraiser.

Together at last, the man and the woman would enjoy eight American grandchildren, four Swedish ones, and some two-hundred African children who know them as *bibi* and *babu*. Together, they would travel the world, plant gardens, create homes in both their countries, and work to remedy the cause and effects of a terrible disease. Together, they would grow into contented old age and ever-deepening love—a love spread over five decades, three continents, and two centuries. A love worth waiting for.

—*Jann Mitchell-Sandstrom*

The Anniversary Gift

"I can't get out of the car!" I yelled.

"Oh, dude, I'm sorry." Jeff walked around the back of the Explorer to the passenger side.

The gash from my C-section ached as I maneuvered out of the open car door. I slid between our car and the one right next to us. Its tires sat on the yellow line.

"It's over the line!" I grumbled.

"I know," Jeff said. "Kel, I could move our car."

"Where?" I said. "The parking garage is full."

He shrugged as I inched my way out, taking his hand. *Happy anniversary*, I thought. Tears threatened, but I held them back. I had cried every day for the last thirty-two days; I did not want to cry today, our tenth anniversary.

Ten years, married to the same person. A milestone. We had planned a trip to relive our honeymoon in Mexico, had made the reservations a year in advance, only to cancel them months before the trip.

"It's safe to say you won't be going," my obstetrician, Dr. Clark, said at my first appointment. "This pregnancy is high risk. There's anywhere from a twelve to fifty percent chance something could go wrong."

I nodded, frowning. I both wanted and feared this pregnancy. My oldest son, Aaron, had been born two and a half months early due to a nasty case of toxemia. For a few days after his birth, it was unclear if either one of us would live.

But we did, and Jeff and I wanted to have another child. We told ourselves that pregnancy is risky no matter what, that we could handle the challenge. The statistics were so broad, there was a good chance this pregnancy would be a smooth experience.

I wasn't sure I ever believed that.

At seven months pregnant, I was admitted to the hospital, just as I had been with my first son. The difference this time was that my placenta had sprung a leak, which put only my second son's life in danger instead of both of our lives.

After twenty-four days trapped in a hospital bed, I gave birth to Noah, who weighed only 4 pounds but was otherwise healthy. However, at two months early, he needed to stay in the Neonatal Intensive Care Unit until he was able to eat on his own.

Jeff and I shuffled toward the elevator, through the skyway and a maze of hallways to another elevator, and finally to the NICU.

Noah slept peacefully, swaddled in a pastel blanket, a hat perched on his tiny head. Around us, monitors attached to all the NICU babies beeped in different pitches, what we joked was the NICU orchestra.

"Can you get the screens?" I asked Jeff.

He nodded, looking around the unit.

A nurse approached. "What are you looking for?"

"Screens to practice breastfeeding," Jeff said.

"For Noah?"

"Yeah."

The nurse looked uncomfortable. "He seemed hungry earlier, so he's been fed. I'm sorry; we didn't know you were coming today."

Jeff and I stood in silence. We journeyed to the NICU each day, making arrangements for our oldest son to stay somewhere while we drove the 15 miles to visit. We tried to time our visits to coincide with feedings, usually the only times Noah was awake.

I sat in the rocking chair Jeff pulled up behind me. I laid my head back and looked up at the ceiling, using gravity to force my tears back. I did not want to cry today. Today, everything was going to be better.

"We can still hold him, though?" I heard Jeff ask.

"Oh, yeah, no problem," the nurse said.

Jeff picked up our tiny son, untangling the cords that measured Noah's vital signs, and laid him in my arms. I put my nose in the crease of his neck and inhaled, nuzzling his cheek next to mine.

Jeff sat across from us in another rocking chair a nurse had pulled up. Halfway through our hour-long visit, I offered him Noah and left to go pump in the NICU's pumping room.

Breastfeeding your baby while not actually having your baby with you is not an easy task. Every two to three hours I would dutifully hook up the breast pump, gather my measly cc's of milk, and refrigerate them until visiting time. I usually needed to pump while at the hospital to cover our travel time.

After my breasts had been tugged empty, I bottled up the breast milk to take to the NICU fridge. It needed to be labeled and placed in a tray with Noah's name on it.

I lined up the bottles on the counter above the refrigerator. There were six three-ounce bottles. None were more than half full. I opened the refrigerator and glanced inside to see several large bottles filled to the top with breast milk. I stared at my bottles. I had fought hard for that milk. I wanted full bottles. *Six half-full bottles will make three full bottles*, I said to myself, twisting the cap off the first two bottles. I turned, knocking the bottles over. My breast milk spread across the counter.

Jeff had come up behind me, ready to go. He stared. First at the puddle, then at my face.

"Just go ahead," Jeff said. He placed a hand on my shoulder. "I'll clean it up."

I nodded. I waited by the nearest elevator, every so often wiping my face on my sleeve.

In silence, we journeyed down the elevator, through the halls, across the skyway, down the other elevator, and into the parking garage.

"Just cry," Jeff said in the darkness of the garage.

"I don't want to! It's our anniversary, and I have makeup on, and I don't sleep, and it's a special day, and we don't even get to do anything really special," I blubbered, my face in my hands, standing beside our car's passenger door.

Jeff hugged me, and I let him, pushing the side of my face against his chest. I breathed in his scent, a mix between the soap and deodorant he's used since I first met him when I was fourteen and he was sixteen. And underneath, that slight musky smell of our adolescence reminded me of our first high school dance, our make-out sessions, and the day we said good-bye when he went off to college. The scent reminded me of the afternoon we got married, when the rhododendrons outside the church bloomed in brilliant fuchsia and delicate violet and the sun warmed us as we drove away together.

"Well," he said.

"Well, what?" I breathed in again.

"Maybe it's not about that."

"About what?" I took another breath.

"Maybe an anniversary isn't about makeup and romance and fancy food. Maybe it's about remembering."

My tears had stopped. "Remembering what?"

"Remembering why we got married in the first place. Remembering to just be here."

Stunned, calmed, I looked up at him.

"So what do we do? For our anniversary?" I asked.

"It doesn't matter," he said. "Are you ready to go?"

I shrugged. "Sure."

As we drove out of the parking garage into the sunlight, I held his hand. Sometimes, that's all you can do. It was the perfect anniversary gift.

—*Kelly Wilson*

Come Rain or Come Shine

"How ya' doin' on this side?" asks my husband, Jean-Marc, as he walks by me with a bucket full of water for the hundredth time.

"I think I just saw an Orca swim by," I tease.

"Tell him to grab a mop and help out."

Usually Tuesdays are fun. Usually on Tuesdays our kids are in school, my husband has the day off, and we indulge in date day. A normal Tuesday date day involves hiking, biking, playing gin rummy, or watching reruns of *Match Game*. But ask anyone in Rhode Island and they'll tell you that Tuesday, March 30, 2010, was anything but normal.

Rhode Islanders had just endured an extremely rainy summer followed by an equally rainy winter. So instead of a spring where snow melted slowly enough to be absorbed into the ground, our yards were saturated. Nine inches of rainfall the week before caused local lakes and rivers to fill to capacity, leaving the seven inches of rainfall to come with nowhere to go.

"Did you know it's raining outside?" Jean-Marc asks rhetorically as he returned to his post on the other side of the basement with his empty bucket.

"Have I mentioned how un-fun this is?" I reply.

"How un-fun is it?" he yells in his best *Match Game* studio-audience voice.

"It's so un-fun that I'd rather be in Cancun!"

Even the sound of the wet vac being turned on doesn't drown out the echo of his laughter.

Fourteen and a half years prior—before marriage, kids, and mortgage—we had been a couple of carefree twenty-something-year-olds living in sin and vacationing in Cancun, Mexico. The trip had been our first "vacation for two" and only my second time outside the United States. For the first two days, Eduardo served us *cervasas* on the beach as we soaked up the sun and booked excursions to local sites.

On day three, the clouds rolled in.

On day four, after the bus dropped us off at an ecological park, the heavens opened up and we wasted seven hours crammed in a gift shop with a hundred other tourists all waiting for the buses to return.

By day six, we had spent all our *pesos* on Doritos, chocolate chip cookies, and Coca Cola, hung the *"No Molestar"* sign on our hotel room door, and watched *muchos* episodes of *Scooby Doo* dubbed in Spanish.

"I can't stand the rain . . ." sings my husband, walking by with another bucket full of Rhode Island rainfall.

I pick up my now-filled tub and follow him up the stairs. "Purple rain, purple rain . . ."

Outside, the storm pelts us from all directions as we let the water gush down our driveway like a double Niagara Falls.

"Raindrops keep falling on my head . . ."

"Red rain is pouring down, pouring down all over me . . ."

"Wait!" cheers Jean-Marc. "I think it's stopped!"

"You're inside again," I tell him.

"I knew it seemed too good to be true."

I lead us back down the stairs, and upon reaching the last step I notice a new little trail of water. "You've got to be kidding me! Another leak?"

My husband kisses my forehead. "By Saturday, it'll be like this never happened."

"Are you insane? If this keeps up, I'll drown by Thursday."

"Turn that frown upside-down, *muchacha*."

"How can you stay so cheery?"

"We survived Cancun, we can survive this. Besides, the newest leak is on your side."

Before I can swat him with a nearby towel, he zips around the corner.

"*Viva Cancun*," my husband shouts as he turns on the wet vac again.

As I use the mop to sop up water from the newest leak, my thoughts return to our last night in Cancun. The loud rain had subsided, the fierce winds had calmed, and for the first time in days, we believed we would finally get a good, albeit lumpy, night's sleep. A couple hours later, however, we both awoke to the rhythmic sound of *drip-drip-drip*.

Clicking on the light, we searched the room for the origin of the noise and found it beginning in the roof and landing directly into Jean-Marc's sneaker. We marveled at Mother Nature's aim and accuracy, then replaced Jean-Marc's sneaker with the room's wastebasket. We snuggled back into bed, clicked out the light, and allowed the drip to lull us back to dreamland.

Drip. Drip. Drip. Splink.

"What the—?"

Another scavenger hunt of the room revealed a second leak, so we utilized the ice bucket to collect those drops. By morning, we had enlisted the help of a second ice bucket, a plastic cup, and a soda bottle to prevent our room from becoming the hotel's first indoor swimming pool. And despite the shining sun, our attention could not be distracted from the numerous overturned lounge chairs, knocked over signs, and uprooted trees.

"*Hola, senorita,*" says Jean-Marc, jolting me back to our present-day flood. "I hope this little *huracan* will not keep you from visiting us again."

I laugh.

Jean-Marc smiles too. "There's the smile I love so much. After you, *gringa.*"

As we lug our buckets up the stairs once more, my husband changes to a French accent. "Oooh la, la! Look at zee *deriere*, de Madame. *Tres mignon.*"

Outside, he switches to English. "Iceberg, dead ahead!"

Inside again, he taps me on the shoulder. "Excuse me, which way to the lido deck?"

"Five fathoms down this way, sir."

We kiss and return to our respective basement posts. As the wet vac drowns out the sound of my husband singing "La Cucaracha" off key, I think of all the storms we've weathered since that trip to Cancun. Planning a wedding. Buying a house.

Post-partum depression. A child with Asperger's syndrome. The passing of Jean-Marc's parents. And though I know these are probably just the tip of the iceberg of what is yet to come, I won't sink into despair. Instead, I'll pick up my mop, sop up some water, squeeze it into the bucket, and know that by this Saturday today's adventure will be just another drop in the bucket. Because the love Jean-Marc and I share is a lifeboat that is strong enough to weather us through any storm together.

—*Judy L. Adourian*

The Taming of the Green-Eyed Monster

Several months ago, my husband of thirty-three years told me, "You have until I'm sixty to stop worrying that I'm going to fall for another woman. No one will want me then." He laughed.

By that time, we will have been married thirty-eight years. John believes it's time I finally trust that he is devoted to me and only me. I agree, but we'll see.

My insecurities probably started as a toddler. Mom tells a story of storming into a lounge, me on her hip, and challenging my father to get off the barstool next to the pretty brunette. "You'd better be home before we get there," she said before storming back out. She'd known my dad would be meeting this woman for a week, and couldn't wait to catch him at it. Dad did beat us home. But he went out and met other women again, and again, and again.

My mother eventually moved him out, into a furnished singles apartment, while he "worked." She hung his clothes in the closet, bought him linens, put sandwich makings into the refrigerator—even stocked the bar. She was still in love with him. And Dad, I remain convinced, was truly in love with her. He would have never moved out on his own. He swore till the day he died that he never "played nookie" with any other woman while he and Mom were together. Mom laughs, "He started fooling around on me while we were in high school. I even broke off our engagement because of it."

John has never done anything that even vaguely resembles the philandering behavior of my father. He doesn't flirt; if he winks or whistles at a woman, it's at me. He refers to me as his girl, calls me "my love," serenades me with Eric Clapton's "Wonderful Tonight." John has never hung out in bars after work; he comes home to me as fast as he can. The only other girl he's really been with is a girl named Cindy. He went with her in high school, not for long, and *he* broke it off. I pried that out of him. I probably shouldn't have, because even after all these years, I think of her whenever I meet somebody named Cindy.

But Cindy is not the only girl I've been jealous of over the years. Heck, girls; I even became jealous of John's guitar. "You touch that guitar more than me," I cried early on in our marriage. Then there were the secretaries. I imagined one had kissed him after I'd matched her kamikaze for kamikaze, me a stay-at-home mom and totally out of practice. John and I were attending his going-away party; he'd been transferred to another department at AiResearch. That was 1981; I may finally be convinced it didn't happen. Another, John hired when he started his moving and storage business. I talked to her on the phone for months before I met her. When I finally saw her in person—oh, my gosh!—she was beautiful.

"But, honey," John explained, "when I hired her she was fat."

My insecurities continue to haunt us. I continue to question John and to size up the women he works with. I wonder if I would have worried less if John had worked at fewer jobs over the years and met fewer women. I doubt it.

Our family, like many others, has been hit by the recession. John has been out of work for much of the past two years. We recently moved from Portland, Oregon, back to Bend, where we feel at home. But I am working, and John is lonely. His music and his guitar (which I now love almost as much as he does) are not enough to fill the empty spots. I have fiddled a bit on Facebook for a year or so, during which John has shown no interest. Whenever I've tried to coax him to join he's always declined.

"But baby—"

"No."

"But your old friends, who you still tell me stories about like it was yesterday—"

"No!"

"Okay," I'd finally give up.

One evening I came home from work, and seeing the slump in his step I decided to pop onto my Facebook account. There, I saw the faces of extended family and friends, many of whom are in California, where we lived till we were in our thirties, and of our children, who are three hours away in Portland. I smiled that rascally smile I attribute to my mother.

"Baby!" I called across our little apartment. I was at the computer in our office; he had stepped into our bedroom. "We're signing you up on Facebook."

"No," he said, as always, but walked into the room. A few minutes later, he was in the chair, looking up friends, and smiling too.

By the next day, he was back in touch with Harold and Jeff, whom he hadn't talked with in fifteen to twenty years, and he was posting back and forth with our family in California and reaching out to our kids and friends in Portland and even friends here in Bend. From then on, I often came home from work to find him on the computer, sometimes laughing out loud. I felt pleased with myself . . . until one night when I walked into the house and saw John standing in the kitchen with a nervous look on his face.

"Honey, I have to tell you something," he said. "I went onto Facebook . . ." And my loving husband proceeded to rattle off his story about how he was looking at a friend's "friends" page and came across a girl named Pauline who had been a friend of his in high school. He wrote her a little note saying, "Hi, it's fun to see your face. You don't have to write me back, just wanted to say hello," something like that; sent it off; decided to look at her "friends" page and saw . . . and here he paused.

"Cindy!" I threw in.

"Yes," he said. "And I didn't feel like I could ignore her without hurting her feelings. So I wrote her the same sort of note, with the 'you don't have to friend me back.' And well, Pauline didn't, but Cindy did."

I kind of laughed, thinking John was pretty cute.

"Let's go look at her!" I said, excited to see what this Cindy looked like.

John and I giggled our way into the office. He pulled up his Facebook account and sat me in the chair. Cindy's picture was off to the left, among

John's cluster of friends. I clicked on it and then clicked on it again to make it bigger.

"Shit! She's hot. And skinny," I said. But I continued to giggle, now because I was a little nervous. "Honey, how fun," I said, trying to be a big girl.

I am fifty-three. John is fifty-five (which means I only have five years to get over this jealousy thing).

John pulled out a blue sticky-note, wrote his Facebook log-in and password on it, and shoved it at me. "You can go on anytime," he insisted.

"Oh, honey, I'm not—" I crushed it in my palm and tossed it into the trashcan without even finishing my sentence.

My cell phone rang. It was our twenty-nine-year-old daughter.

"Hey, go onto Facebook," I told her. "You can see Daddy's old girlfriend. She's hot. And she's skinny."

As you've probably figured out, I am not skinny, for sure. I weigh forty pounds more than when John and I got married. But he thinks I'm hot and tells me often.

Over the next few days, I continued to tell close friends and family to take a peek at Cindy on John's Facebook page. And then I let it go, truly . . . until I walked into the apartment after a very rough day at work and John quickly turned off the computer. *Cindy!* is where my mind went. Embarrassed, I kept my mouth shut.

John stood, greeted me with a hug, and then while pouring me a glass of chardonnay said he had chicken and broccoli ready for me. John has been doing most of the cooking since he's been out of work. Sometimes it's breakfast while I'm getting ready for work; sometimes a sack lunch; and often dinner, which he keeps warm if I work late. This was a late night, so he had already eaten. He sat and visited with me while I ate my warmed dinner at the kitchen table, patient with me as I shared my day.

I decided to finish my wine while checking my e-mail. John went into the living room to catch up on what was happening with the NCAA's "March Madness" on TV. E-mail-schmemail; I went straight to Facebook, to John's wall, and stared at Cindy. I turned off the computer, fast. Went in and sat right next to my husband on our big ol' couch.

"We've got a problem," I said.

John paused his recorded basketball game.

"Honey, I'm jealous of Cindy. It wouldn't be so hard if she wasn't so pretty," I said . . . okay, whined.

"I'll just block her," he said.

"No, you can't do that."

"I knew this could be a problem. I'll close my Facebook account."

"No. You're having so much fun with it," I said. "I'm sorry. But you being friends with Cindy feels dangerous to me."

John stiffened, feeling like I'd questioned his trustworthiness. "I'm going to take her off there," he repeated.

"Let me sleep on it," I said. After all, I'd had a really tiring day. And I'd just talked to a married girlfriend who has been looking at an old (also married) boyfriend's Facebook wall wondering if he is intending to send her secret messages through his posts, a conversation I'd neglected to share with John.

He reluctantly agreed to wait.

In the morning, after waking to several bad dreams during the night, I got up and walked straight into the office. I turned on the computer, then picked through the trashcan, unfolding every little blue note I could find without making too much noise. With no password found and horrified that John would hear me if I dumped the entire contents onto the floor, I went back to the bedroom. The sun was coming up, and John was stirring.

"Honey."

"Uh-huh," he answered.

"I'm still having a hard time with this Cindy thing."

"I will get her off there today."

"Thanks, baby," I said, climbing into bed with him. "I'm really sorry."

John held me, hugged me, and kissed me on the forehead.

That day while I was at work, John wrote to Cindy and explained to her, honestly, like I encouraged him to do, that his wife is a jealous lunatic (in so many words). When I got home, he relayed to me that she understood, that her husband works with a lot of "hot, young babes" and it bothers her, but she's never told him.

"Give your wife a hug for me," she'd said.

"Damn," I said, "she's even nice."

So is my husband, especially to me. And he loves me, only me, for eternity. I have five more years to *get* that . . . and to get over this jealousy thing. He may have to extend that deadline.

—*Ande Cardwell*

Three Little Words

In the beginning, three little words followed us everywhere we went. To the movies. Restaurants. That silly beach bar where the guitar player strummed Jimmy Buffett songs. Even down by the river, where we walked each night, jeans rolled up to our knees, hands lightly touching. Three little words.

I love you.

They were there on our wedding day with fifty people drinking mimosas at 11:00 A.M. as the river-boat sauntered down the coast. Paddlewheel churning. Wedding guests laughing. A singer crooning "Unforgettable." We danced so close I could feel your warm breath like fingers on the back of my neck.

I love you.

They were even there when you carried me over the threshold into our new cookie-cutter house. Magnolia trees dotted the lawns, and everyone had matching black mailboxes with little red flags. Perfect, we thought.

I love you.

The children came soon after that. A boy first, quiet and cuddly. Then a girl, colicky, screaming even as you swaddled her. The words still came back then. But they didn't show up as often anymore. When they did, they sounded weary and spent and muttered into a pillow case.

I . . . love . . . you.

I don't know when it happened really. There wasn't a particular moment in time. But one day I noticed the words were gone. Not completely. But gone like old friends who'd moved away, promising to come back and visit. Just as soon as soccer season ended. Or a work deadline passed. Or someone got over the flu. It's amazing how life can hum along even without old friends. Without those three little words.

We moved into a bigger house, a two-story with ivy that scaled the red brick. You liked the game room upstairs and talked about adding a pool table and shooting eight-ball on Friday nights. But that was before the kids filled the room with their roller blades and bicycle helmets and video play stations. Soon the pool table became just another one of those things that parents dream about, like uninterrupted sleep or car seats without Cheerios stuffed in the cracks.

You started to spend a lot of time working outside, baking in the Florida heat, edging the corners of our lawn into perfect 90-degree angles. That's when the new words started to come around. Curious, at first. A little too friendly. Like uninvited neighbors. They'd watch while you power-washed the driveway and sheared the ivy from the brick. Three new words.

He's a keeper.

I'd nod in agreement. They were right, after all. I'd let those new words sit for a while, sipping lemonade, talking about the weather. I'd try to get comfortable with them, to make them feel at home. Then something would interrupt the lazy afternoon. A child's splinter. A phone ringing. Our dog busting out the front door. I'd have to excuse myself and bolt down the block, because Mrs. Reilly had taken out her broom already and was getting dangerously close to the terrier squatting on her front lawn. I'd run in circles trying to catch that crazy dog. Just when I was almost ready to let Mrs. Reilly take a whack at him, you'd come running up behind me. Leash in hand. Pieces of ivy still stuck to your arms.

He's a keeper.

So I let the new words in. I got comfortable with them. Over time, I came to appreciate their steadiness. Their predictability. The way they never let me down. Even though they didn't sparkle or take my breath away.

Years passed. Jobs came and went. We dished out money for pre-paid college plans and two sets of braces, for horseback riding lessons and broken arms, and for 2,041 teenage text messages. And long after we'd accepted that these comfortable words were enough, that it was okay that the "I love yous" only wanted to come around for birthdays and anniversaries . . . we got the call.

Nobody is prepared for that call. Nobody can imagine what it's like to lay on that cold, metal table day after day. To wait for the buzzer to sound and for beams of radiation to pass through tight red skin. Nobody is prepared for the surgery, either. To lose a piece of herself. To feel that sharp twinge in those last fleeting moments just before unconsciousness, when every fiber pulses with the same three words.

I'm not ready!

You were at my bedside when I awoke. Holding my hand. Stroking my hair. You pretended not to notice when the bandages came off, when it became obvious that even with reconstructive surgery, I would never look exactly the same again. That's when you kissed me, right there in the hospital, right at the very moment when I felt the most unkissable. And that's when I knew. Three new words.

I need you.

As I healed, you learned how to cook chicken paprikash. To shuttle kids to band practice. To fold laundry into neat, fluffy stacks. You learned how to correct algebra problems. To write limericks. To braid a girl's hair. And to my surprise, you learned when to draw back the shades and tell me about all those little things that happened during the day. And when to say nothing at all.

I need you.

In time, I grew strong again. Strong enough to reclaim my place, to fall back into my old routine. But as I did, I began to notice something: How wonderful bakery bread smelled. How winning a game of Yahtzee could make me feel good all day long. How everything that had seemed so dull and tedious before seemed to sparkle now.

That discovery made me want to take a walk with you. A walk down by the river, with jeans rolled up to our knees, hands lightly touching. I could feel the sun's warmth slipping away and the soft moss beneath my feet. You stopped to skip a stone across the glassy water. That's when our eyes met, so much older now, wrinkled at the corners by every twist and turn of life. For a moment, the wind seemed to still. The leaves hushed. Songbirds quieted. It was as if they were all watching and waiting . . . wanting the words to come. Those three little words.

But instead you took my hand and we walked away in silence, past the crook where we used to stop, farther than we'd ever gone before. We walked without words because the silence seemed to be enough. Because all the growing and changing and accepting had made our love become something more than three little words.

So much more.

—Madeleine M. Kuderick

When His and Hers Becomes Ours

Last year, after ten years of dating, my boyfriend moved in with me. Our respective children are nearly out of the house or about to leave. They've been alternately amusing and needy, lovely and obstinate, fun and exhausting, and now it's time for us. Yes, we're finally having our own grown-up adventure.

Make that groan up.

You never get the full flavor of someone's personality until you're sharing the same space—linen closet, bathtub, packed-to-the-gills garage, mailbox, and recycling bins—24/7.

After fifteen years on my own following a divorce, I'm sharing space again with a man: a small ranch with galley kitchen, a combined living/dining area, and a master bedroom no bigger than some friends' mud rooms.

Tonight, I'm holed up in my daughter's former bedroom, now my study, because I'm mad at my guy. Usually, he's thoughtful and considerate. He brings me coffee every morning, calls me at work daily, and does the food shopping, a task he knows I dislike. He's patient to a fault and a great listener. Yes, he's a catch. So what's the catch?

He can be inflexible. He's a neatnik who likes to point out others' messes. He gets angry and won't talk; in other words, he's perfected the art of stone-walling. It's a tricky, sometimes dangerous, trifecta.

Tonight, he's accused me once again of making a muddle of the kitchen cabinet above our sink. True, I've sneaked back in the set of bright orange plastic drinking glasses he hates, strewn matchbooks and incense sticks all over, and—I freely admit—defiantly placed, front and center on the bottom shelf, a jar of honey-mustard pretzel-dipping sauce he explicitly said to toss. The offending jar, nothing we'll ever use, is the first thing you spot when opening the cabinet door.

"I see you've made a mess of this again," he said earlier while dishing up some leftovers. A casual comment, perhaps, but it got my goat.

So here I sit, steaming, thinking about that old truism of relationships: Something I once found endearing about this man—his sock-sorting,

pillow-plumping, silverware-straightening penchant for order—is the very same thing that
makes me crazy now.

Living together means sharing household items,
easier promised than practiced. Take last winter.
There we were, nestled by the fire on a snowy evening. My partner lay on the couch, my feet in his
lap. The television clicker was positioned in hand.

His hand.

He clicked us through a parade of news, ice-
skating and HGTV shows, and a *Gilligan's Island*
rerun. When the Bette Midler tearjerker, *Beaches*,
flashed on screen, I yelled, "Stop!" And then, the
four words that strike the most fear in a man's heart:
"Give me the clicker."

To my astonishment, he kept clicking.

"You're not going to give it to me?" I said, where-
upon, smiling Cheshire Cat-like, he strengthened his
grip around the black device.

"What do you need it for?" he asked, his knuckles
turning a paler shade of white.

I saw, in that moment, a side of my loving,
evolved, progressive guy I'd rarely seen: Cro-Magnon.
I was suddenly reminded of the fact that in the first
photo I ever took of him, he was curled in a club
chair, clicker in hand.

I rustled myself out of my sleepy position. "I want it."

"Why?" he asked this time.

I could feel my anger grow as I watched him clutch the plastic gadget even tighter. I never knew he had such strong palm control or such dogged determination about matters so inconsequential. Disgusted, I got up and stalked off to the bedroom, to another TV and a clicker of my own.

He thought I was being childish. I thought him unreasonable and, well, controlling.

Stalemate.

A part of me feels foolish even mentioning our remote-control tiff. Eventually, we talked. We walked it off. We laughed. Some relationships sizzle, some offer an oasis of calm. Ours? It's true that when we click, we click. He made a peace offering of the remote every night after that. (*Beaches*, anyone?)

Living together means sharing decisions. Again, easier said than done; easier when you are in two separate houses, his and yours. Harder when you're both living in yours and you've got an old swimming pool that neither of you uses or wants to maintain.

The pool liner is leaking; the cover is ancient. It's time for a little TLC. Or is it? It will cost us thousands to get the pool looking spanking new and working flawlessly again. Clearly, my swimming pool and I have arrived at that point where all complicated relationships end up sooner or later: commit to the long haul or break up.

Despite the costs, I would like to keep the pool. After fourteen years together, we've got history. My partner thinks otherwise. He promises me apple and pear trees, flowering bushes, a deck, if only I'd agree to excavate. He'll build me a little cottage-studio where I can make art, or perhaps we could enjoy some other form of luxurious liquid, like a pond with fish, Japanese water garden, or fountain.

"Don't rule those out; they are beautiful," he says, upping the ante in his efforts to change my mind.

"We'll see," I say. I can stonewall, too.

Living together means sharing the thing that enlarges the more you give it away: love. And there are many ways to demonstrate it.

"Remind me to put a jacket on the water heater," my guy says, stepping out of the shower, which, he notes, is running tepid.

I wait a beat for the follow-up wisecrack, the punch line, the laugh at my expense. We are hopeless kidders. But his face is so open; his tone, guileless. He isn't joking.

Forget the roses, the Riesling, the Lucinda Williams tickets. (Well, don't forget them entirely.) I thrill to the thought of my partner rushing out to Home Depot to find the perfect wrap for the tank that will give us a stream of continuous, hot water.

In these tough times, is this the new language of love?

Later that evening, while we're at an antiques auction, he returns to the topic. "Maybe you'll help me pick out the water heater jacket." He nudges his seat closer to mine. "They have different types, you know."

"They do?" Okay, now he's pulling my leg.

Up front, the stern auctioneer with the ricochet voice is belting out prices, trying to coax the crowd to bid on drop-leaf tables, brass footstools, art deco ashtrays.

"Really," my guy says.

"They don't," I insist.

"Plaid."

"They make Burberry jackets for water heaters?"

My guy smiles. I smile back. My thoughts are warm and cozy.

In another lifetime, another partner, this one a husband, wrapped me in mink. But this seemed to have everything to do with him, nothing to do with me. Status.

Don't get me wrong, I took the fur and wore it for years before my conscience kicked in. I sold it for a fair price to a stranger with cancer who said she wanted to own a fur coat before she died.

But wrapping the water heater has everything to do with me and the man in my life, and more importantly, with us.

Living together means planning for the future. Last weekend, at another auction, we bought a set of mid-century Adirondack twig furniture—beautiful settee, two matching chairs, and a table—for the house in the mountains we don't own but might some day.

Being coupled means taking a leap of faith, even when you feel the other person is cramping your style. And learning that love can thrive in that slippery, uncomfortable space between feeling stuck and preparing to soar.

—Tina Lincer

As Long as Forever

Wearing an old black overcoat to warm his frail body, an argyle sock on one foot and a black dress sock on the other, Dad leaned forward in his easy chair, staring disconsolately around him. "I'm looking for something," he told me.

"What is it, Dad?"

"Well, it's about this big," he began, raising a hand up from the ground, "and it's hard to describe, but . . . well, I can't quite get a hold of the, the . . ."

"The name of what it is?" I wondered aloud.

"Yes. What is the problem? I need to know."

He got up and began wandering about, through the kitchen, past the couch, back to his chair, and stopping when he was once again in the kitchen. Then he walked back to his easy chair again.

"Did you remember what you're looking for, Dad?"

"It's just that I need to experiment so I can think. I can't think, for some reason."

"Do you need me to get you something, Dad? Maybe a snack?"

"No. I'm not hungry. Well . . . yes, I need something, but what is it? I don't remember. It's so irritating when I don't remember."

I sighed, wishing I could do something to help him. I was babysitting Dad for my mother, his main caregiver. Dad has Alzheimer's, and Mom can't get away to do anything unless someone can watch him. That night, she had to spend the night at a hospital for a sleep test, so I stayed with him—my first time spending the night at my parents' home in years.

"Dad, maybe you're looking for Mom?"

"Yes, that's it! Where is she?"

"She's at the hospital getting a test. She asked me to stay here with you so she could go get the test because she needs to find out what's wrong to get better medicine. She'll be back in the morning."

"That's good," he said. "But it causes a problem for me. I have to call someone to come pick me up."

"Dad, if someone takes you somewhere, you won't be here when Mom gets home and she won't know where you are."

"Oh, yeah. Well, I guess I'm just stuck with a problem then."

He walked around the island separating the living room from the kitchen and rummaged around in a drawer for a few minutes. I heard him mutter, "A tablespoon. That will do." Then he went over to the cupboards. There, he pulled out some napkins and paper towels and headed over toward me.

"What are those for, Dad?"

"I have to think. If I do this thing . . . what is it called . . . I can't think of the word . . ."

"You mean experiment?"

"An experiment. Yes, that's what it's called. If I do that, then I can think."

He sat down, pulled two handkerchiefs out of his pocket, and became absorbed in arranging all the stuff he had together on a round lamp table next to his chair.

I began thinking about one night when I was around sixteen. I'd been crying because a boy had broken up with me, and Dad hugged me tight.

"Dad, why can't things be easy?" I'd sobbed. "All I want is to be happy."

He had replied, "I know, honey. It hurts, but in time things will be okay. You'll meet the right man, one who will love you forever, and you'll forget the pain."

"When you met Mom, did you love her forever?"

"Ah, your mother." I watched his face as a look of satisfaction washed over it. "Yes, I was nineteen at the time. I went to a youth group at church, and I saw her and thought, 'Wow!' I asked my friend who she was. He told me her name was Marilyn and she was only fourteen. I said, 'I'm going to marry that girl someday.'

"I had to go into the Navy right after that, because the war started," he continued. "So I waited until she was sixteen. Then I wrote to the leader of the youth group, asking if she'd have Marilyn write to me to tell me news of home. We wrote pretty regularly for the next two years. When I got out of the service, she was eighteen, and I asked her to marry me then and there. I've been in love with her since she was fourteen, and I'll love her until the day I die."

Somehow, the thought of his undying love for my mother helped, and my tears had dried up, for the moment, way back then. But now . . .

I watched Dad fold the napkins, paper towels, and handkerchiefs into two lumpy white piles, then carefully place two silver tablespoons upon the piles. He laid one spoon on a napkin pile at the right side of the lamp neck, the other spoon on a napkin pile mirroring it on the left. He turned off the lamp, turned it back on, then picked up the spoons and moved the piles of napkins so they formed two long piles with two shorter piles at one end of each pile. Then he laid the spoons gently down on the longer piles, with the bowls of the spoons on the two shorter piles, still separated by the lamp's neck. Once again, he turned the light off and on, staring intently at the spoons as if he expected something to happen.

"Dad, are you okay?"

"Yes, I'm fine. I just have to think, you see? Doing these . . . I can't think, you know . . . so doing these . . ."

"Experiments?" I suggested.

"Yes. Doing experiments helps me think."

He picked up everything off the lamp table and reorganized it again.

Poor Dad. He used to be a scientist, so now he makes up pretend experiments. It's so awful; he can't think or talk about things. Poor Mom. She has to watch him all the time. She never gets a break, never gets to go places, and hardly gets to visit with people outside church on Sunday. I wish we didn't live over 200 miles away. But when she was leaving to go to the hospital for her test, she'd told him, with shaking voice, "I know I'm going to miss you, because I miss you already and I'm not even gone yet! But I'll be home soon."

My soul cried out for help, for something that could take away the hard times and help my mom and dad to be happy.

Dad continued playing with his napkin piles and spoons for over an hour while I read a book, waiting for him to get sleepy and want to go to bed.

Finally, I said, "Dad, it's after eleven-thirty. Don't you want to go to sleep?"

"Can't go to sleep. No. There's more people involved now."

"Do you mean Mom? She'll be home soon." I explained, once again, how she was at the hospital getting a test and would be home tomorrow morning. "Are you sure you don't want to go to bed?"

"No, I don't. I want to get a feeling for things," he replied. "With my . . ."

"Experiments," I whispered, as he began moving the piles and the spoons around again, turning the light on and off again, and staring hard at them as if something in this setup would solve the problem of Mom's being gone overnight.

Dad's head began to droop, and soon his chin rested on his chest. As he started breathing more slowly and regularly, I went to let the dog out. When I opened the front door, Dad jumped up and walked quickly over to me.

"I have a problem, and I need someone to help me," Dad said, in an uncharacteristically shaky voice, his eyes brimming with tears. His face somehow reminded me of a lost little boy.

Gently, I asked, "Dad, do you need a hug?"

"No. I need help is all. But I can't remember what it's about."

"Is it because Mom's gone?"

"That's it!"

I explained it once more. His voice still shook a little, but he agreed that it was good she was getting a test. He walked back to his easy chair and sat down.

Dad picked up the spoons, pushed all the napkins together in one big pile, and set the spoons right next to each other on the pile of napkins, stared at it with a smile, and turned off the light. Then his face went blank, and in the dim light from the lamp near me I watched as, again, he took the spoons off the big pile and divided up the napkins into two piles.

"Dad, what are the tablespoons for?" I finally asked.

"They represent who lives at this house. There are two of us who live here. And one is gone," he said. "You see my problem? The equation won't work."

I felt my throat squeeze in on itself. The piles of napkins and handkerchiefs were beds, pillows, and blankets. The spoons were Dad and Mom.

He moved the spoons and piles apart, divided by the lamp neck once again, then put them together again, trying to see what he could do to stop the pain of being unable to be with the one he loved. He couldn't understand it, he couldn't explain it, and he was doing his best, in his own world, to try and resolve the problem.

Tears spilled as I said, "Well, Dad, I know Mom loves you, too. And she'll be back in the morning."

Dad took the spoons and tied them with the handkerchiefs, over his mismatched socks, to his feet.

"Dad, it's almost midnight. Do you want to go to bed?"

"No. I'll wait."

He sat on his easy chair again and leaned back; soon his head drooped and a quiet snore drifted out. He couldn't have been comfortable at all, with his clothes still on, with his feet tied up in handkerchiefs and spoons, and with nothing but the thin overcoat to keep him warm. I covered him with a blanket and lay down on the couch. I wouldn't wake him. After all, if a man loves a woman as long as forever, he might at least be allowed to wait for her in the room closest to where she'll return in the morning, so they can be happy together once more.

—*Suzanne Endres*

The Almost-Proposal

Sam and I aren't married yet. We will be married some day; we just aren't married yet. We haven't even discussed marriage. I'm in no hurry. He's in no hurry. Things are good. Things are so good Sam has moved in. I'm happy. He's happy. His cats are happy. My dog is happy. The bills are paid. The refrigerator is full. The sky is blue. Life is good.

But there is a little problem: marriage is on Sam's mind. I seem to be oblivious to his hints. We are still learning about each other, and I can't always tell what he's thinking. I am in love and thrilled that our relationship is so easy.

We've both arranged for the same vacation time and have planned our first trip together. Our itinerary is to drive through New York State to Niagara Falls, then up to Toronto, south through the Thousand Islands area, and back to New Jersey through the Finger Lakes. I'm thinking of it as a romantic adventure with Sam; Sam is looking at it as a pre-honeymoon, and I miss all the signals.

I have not yet developed the intuition of a wife or mother. That comes with time and stretch marks. I know nothing about signs, hunches, or gut feelings. Things don't gnaw at me yet. Things don't play themselves over and over in my mind until I have to wake Sam in the middle of the night because something pissed me off six hours earlier. That will come later. Now, Sam has a plan, and I'm lost in dense fog as we head north to our winter wonderland.

When we leave for our trip, snow is piled on the side of roads and salt stains are on cars. Our heavy jackets are thrown onto the back seat, and the heater is roaring inside the car. Yet, I am so oblivious to Sam's plan that traveling *north* in the *winter* to *Canada* where it is *cold* doesn't even make me raise an eyebrow. We are headed in the general direction of Niagara Falls. Our plan is to drive through the New York side and then to Niagara Falls, Ontario. Sam is driving; I'm navigating.

For the record, Niagara Falls are blow-your-eardrums-out loud. As you approach Niagara Falls, you can hear the thunder of water pushing off a mountain and crashing onto the rocks below. They are raging loud. Imagine trying to talk while a subway screams past you in your living room. I have read that people who are deaf can feel Niagra's vibrations.

When Sam pulls over and says I picked the wrong turn-off, I tell him I didn't.

He sits there with Niagara Falls booming behind him and screams, "You missed the turn! You are not always right, you know!"

I look up from the map, amazed. "Don't you hear anything?" I scream calmly.

"Give me the map," he says.

"You are ridiculous," I reply, cupping my hands over my ears.

"You know, I was going to propose to you this week, but I don't think I can live with such a know-it-all," he mumbles, loud enough for me to hear.

Five minutes later, we are driving past Niagara Falls and Sam is saying, "I knew we were almost here."

In the winter, Niagara Falls has a different appearance than it does on postcards and in travel brochures. The water freezes, forming beautiful ice creations on many precipices. There are also no tourists—except us.

Something else is very different, too. Now I know Sam's ulterior motive for the trip. Sam has, in his moment of moronic rage, spilled the beans. I'm not sure if Sam remembers what he said in his side-of-the-road temper tantrum, but I certainly do. Suddenly, to me, this trip is different. Before, I was traveling with my boyfriend, my roommate, my best friend. Now I'm with someone who wants to live with me for better or for worse, forever after, until death us do part. Before I was relaxed; now I'm wheezing.

We check into our motel. On the surface, everything looks acceptable. It looks clean and things match. I am afraid to look under the bed. I will not stretch out on the carpet to do my sit-ups, but walking across it doesn't seem to be too disgusting as long as I have on shoes.

As I get farther into the room, I notice the picture over the bed, a print of a hill and a field, and in the distance Niagara Falls. It makes sense that they put a picture of Niagara Falls in a room near Niagara Falls. I'm imagining the exact same picture hangs in every room in this motel when I notice something strange about our picture—dirt or something is in the field below the hill. I put on my glasses to get a better look. It seems some previous resident took a pencil to this picture and added little X-rated stick figures, tiny characters doing things in positions that defy gravity and the laws of science. There are anatomically gifted male stick figures and well-endowed female stick figures frolicking on a hillside near

Niagara Falls, their exaggerated teeny-tiny privates sticking way out. Discovering the stick figures puts Sam and me in better moods. We're laughing, and he's my best friend again. We forget the side-of-the-road argument. We are both hungry.

I decide to take a quick hot bath to warm up. Sam turns on the TV to check out Canadian broadcasts. Sam cannot be in a room without a TV on. It is still the first thing he does when he comes home from work. The TV runs constantly in our home, even when there is no one in the room. I walk through the house turning off the unwatched televisions, only to find them on again five minutes later, once again with no one watching them.

I wash the motel bathtub using a lot of disinfectant. I fill the tub and add the scented bubble bath I brought with me. I pile my hair high on my head and slip in. My eyes are closed as I soak and relax. Then it happens.

"Honey?" says Sam, standing in the doorway. He is not in the bathroom or the bedroom but sort of halfway here and halfway there with his eyes on the TV.

"What, Sam?"

"Want to get married?" Now, this is said with the same type of romance as "honey, I'm going down the hall to get a bucket of ice" or "honey, when was the last time you had the oil changed in the Toyota?" He is not even in the room. He is in the stupid doorway. He is not even looking at me. He is looking at a rerun of *One Day at a Time*.

"I'm in the tub, Sam!"

"Oh, okay," he replies.

He plops down on the bed and continues to watch TV while I bathe.

I sit in the tub contemplating what just happened. Sam's romantic nature may be stretching itself to the limit at this point. Then again, I could be hallucinating.

A little while later, we are at the motel's restaurant. Everything matches here, too. Tables match the carpet. Carpet matches the window treatment. Window treatment matches the waitresses' uniforms. In fact, the colors are identical to our room. There is even the same painting over our table—although it lacks the anatomically gifted stick figures. We both notice it. It's the level of cleanliness in this place that worries me. I mention this to Sam.

"I know it isn't your mother's kitchen," he says. "Jeez. Stop being such a clean freak. We're on vacation."

So I go with the punches. To be safe, I stick with something basic to eat: grilled cheese, fries, Diet Coke. Sam orders baby back ribs, the all-you-can-eat special.

"Are you sure?" I ask Sam.

"I'm starved. I haven't eaten since New Jersey."

Fact of significance: Sam finishes not only one large rack, but two and a half large racks of ribs. My comment that the ribs look a little funny—a little green—doesn't impair his appetite.

Then the romantic side of Sam once again shifts into overdrive. Sam decides we should go for a walk to work off the meal and to see Niagara Falls. Sam nixes my idea of driving over. We walk a few blocks. The closer we get to the falls, the louder it gets, the windier it gets, the colder it gets. Sam mentions something about having an upset stomach. I tell him he ate too much. The more we walk, the colder and crankier I get.

I see the falls. It looks like Niagara Falls, only semi-frozen. It's getting dark. Sam snaps some pictures with me and Niagara. I snap a few of Sam and Niagara. No one else is there to preserve this moment of the two of us together in one picture with Niagara Falls behind us. No one is crazy enough to visit Niagara Falls at this time of year, this time of day, in this ridiculous cold. I begin to worry about frostbitten appendages. All I want is to get back to the motel to soak in another hot tub and warm up. My ears hurt. My feet hurt. My toes hurt. My fingers hurt. I am imagining blackened toes. My nostrils are frozen together. I am not in a good mood.

At this point, romantic Sam, yelling over Niagara's rage, chooses to ask me once more, "Wanna get married?"

I look at him. I am sure I heard him right this time. First, he threatens not to propose while we fight about directions to Niagara Falls. Next, he proposes from the doorway while he's still watching TV and I'm taking a bath. And now, while I am freezing alive in subzero weather with my nostrils frozen shut causing me to nearly suffocate, he proposes once again. I have to answer him, but my teeth are chattering. It hurts when the air goes down my windpipe. My eyes are tearing. Icicles are forming on my cheeks and they are not from the classic tears of joy one might expect. I'm thinking that this is about as romantic as Sam can muster: Niagara Falls in the background, the two of us together on vacation, a run-of-the-mill motel room with pornographic pencil drawings above the bed's headboard.

As I'm about to chatter out an answer, Sam loses all the color in his face. He turns bright green and vomits over the railing into the frozen Niagara Falls below. Then he vomits some more. He vomits all the way back to the motel, all through the night, and never again asks me to marry him.

The ten-day trip that we so diligently planned suddenly comes to a screeching halt. We are heading home to New Jersey. Sam is too sick to have fun. I am driving with Sam stretched out on the back seat, groaning. And now I am angry.

Before this trip I hadn't given a single thought to getting married. Now Sam has put the thought in my head and cruelly pulled it off life support. All the way home, I'm incredibly angry with Sam. In my mind, I replay the scene of him calling me a clean freak. Then I replay him vomiting over the railing into the pounding waters of Niagara. I even embellish the story by having the vomit freeze midway down before it hits the water below. I have hundreds of miles to drive and aggravate myself about my almost-proposal. I mumble under my breath while Sam writhes in self-inflicted pain. I have no pity. I manage to drive on every torn-up road from Canada to New Jersey, and I speed joyfully over every speed bump. I deliberately swerve and take corners on two wheels.

Twenty-five years later, I still remind Sam that I never actually said yes to any of his proposals. Then I suggest going out for ribs.

—Felice Prager

This story was first published in *Sasee Magazine*, April 2010, under the title "Waiting for the Right Answer."

Built with Tender Loving Care

Boxes of half-finished stories almost floated out of the storage loft. My files labeled "Miscellaneous Writing Ideas" danced their way to the front of the old file cabinet.

No more red ink. No more late nights writing encouraging comments on student papers, from nervous Laotians to anxious middle-aged men newly laid off from a factory closing. I was done. Though I had loved my teaching job, it had taken its toll and I was worn out. My brain felt worn out. Now, my time was my own. Retirement! Plus, our two children were grown and had left the nest.

Life, fate, whatever you call it, has a way of interrupting one's plans, and just as my dream was unfolding, my husband decided to retire, too, and to pursue his dream of developing lots. He wanted to build a house "on spec," as it's called. We had more land than we needed and through the years had talked of doing this, but it had always seemed just a distant idea. Now, here he was, at the kitchen table—barely past the last toast at his own retirement party—making concrete plans to start cutting trees and grading a road for the first lot.

"I don't want to build any more houses," I told him. "I plan to write stories, to work on a romance novel. I've built and remodeled enough houses to last a lifetime." I meant it.

"You don't have to help," he said. He meant it.

In a matter of weeks, two carpenter relatives were living in our basement in a rough apartment of sorts. Another young man from the neighborhood also moved in. He was in a tough position and needed work, so we willingly hired him.

Do the math: I now had four men to cook for . . . *if* I wanted to do the cooking. This didn't count the extra sheets, towels, and bathrooms to keep clean . . . *if* I wanted that job. It didn't include the extra floor cleaning work, all those muddy boots. And it didn't account for the extra groceries and preparations and clean-up chores . . . *if* I wanted to do any of that.

I suppose I could have refused. But I love my husband and I knew (more than he did) that four men building a house all day need food. They need coffee, coffee cake, meat, and potatoes. They need towels and soap and bathrooms. They need a bed with clean sheets. They need lemonade and ice water.

So it began. I packed up my writing files, walked away from my old desk, and turned off my dream.

"This will last only a few weeks," my husband said.

It didn't take him long to see that "feeding the men" was an important task. "I'd really appreciate it," he said. "It's hard for me to come back and start thinking of something to make for them when they're already hungry." (Not to mention that he was starving too.)

So I did the work that women all over the world do—invisible duties, often taken for granted. I'm not complaining, really. I'm just stating a fact. It's the adage of "someone's got to do it," I guess. And unless you can afford to hire a maid and a cook, that someone is usually the woman of the house.

The first summer went by. I was up before everyone else, making coffee, oatmeal, toast, juice, sometimes eggs. The four men left in two pickups, roared out of the driveway and up to the building site— well-rested, well-fed, ready for a good day's work. I cleaned up the breakfast meal and usually started right in on baking something, a cake or some cookies.

At 10:00 A.M., I showed up at the site with an overflowing picnic basket, warm coffee cake or oatmeal cookies, and more coffee. They had a fifteen-minute break under one of the shade trees.

Back to the house I went and started the noon meal preparations. This included potatoes, meat, a vegetable, and often some kind of dessert. Then they drove back—hot, sweaty, tired—wiping their faces and glancing toward the stove on their way to the bathroom to clean up. They ate lunch, relaxed a bit on the deck, and then went back to work.

As mid-afternoon rolled around, I filled the picnic basket again, this time with something like fruit or more cookies, maybe some milk or soda. Another short break and they'd return to work again.

Back at the house, I started planning the evening meal. This was usually a lighter fare, perhaps a casserole or a pasta dish, maybe some homemade soup and a salad.

I cleaned up and did dishes while the four men sat on the deck and talked, played cards, and made phone calls for the next day's delivery of lumber or cement or gravel. They were all deeply tired and went to bed early.

In between cooking and cleaning up the kitchen, I managed trips to the grocery store, made beds, did laundry, and paid the bills. Then I cooked and cleaned. Cooked and cleaned some more. By the time evening came, I was too tired to do any more than watch the evening news before I fell into bed myself. My days passed like that. Day after day after day.

After two years, the house and a large attached garage were finished. The other men left and went back to their own lives. My husband and I began the tedious work of painting interior walls and finishing the wood trim. He did major landscaping, and I helped sow grass seed and picked rocks. The house was a beautiful cedar-sided two-story with a wrap-around deck and a walk-out basement. We found a Realtor who helped us sell it within six months of it being on the market.

My husband's endeavor was successful. He began talking about the next house he wanted to build.

I was two years into retirement and hadn't written one story or article.

My resentment was palpable. Not only had I not followed my dream, but what I thought had been a generous offer—a willingness to be the helpmate—was now being taken for granted. My cooking and cleaning services were now a "given." Instead of being a writer, I was now the support staff for my husband's projects.

We also had grown apart with the presence of others in the house so often. He was happier laughing and working with the other men than he was taking me out for a movie and a dinner date. He was always too preoccupied and tired. When we did manage time away, all he could talk about was the next house. I just stared out the window.

I became distant and cold. He felt it; I felt it.

"I don't care," I said out loud.

Time passed, and fate had another plan in store for me. My mother suffered a heart attack and underwent triple bypass surgery in a medical center far from our home. I was the sibling most able to help with her long (successful!) recovery, so I went to stay with her for about six months. In some strange way, I was almost relieved to get away from my own home, from my husband, and from the constant pressure of his projects.

My mother grew stronger, and little by little my caretaking skills improved. We'd never been very close, and this turned out to be a special time, when she could count on me and I could nurture her back to health. I took her to her doctor appointments, cooked the right kind of meals for her, and made sure she got to the rehab clinic for her exercises, and we shared many fierce Scrabble games during peaceful winter afternoons. I took long walks when I could and did some hard thinking about my marriage, how lonely I felt, and what I wanted to do in my retirement years. Support staff was not in the cards, and that was kind of scary. I didn't want to go home.

The time came when I was no longer needed at my mother's house. She was well enough to get back to her own life, and I had to face the music at my own house. I hoped to negotiate with my husband for the type of life I wanted and needed. I needed him to see that I had my own dream. He would just have to hire a cook and a cleaner if he was going to continue down this building path. It would be hard to tell him, because I knew that he had a dream too. But it wasn't working for me.

When I walked in the door, he was waiting for me with an unreadable look on his face. "I missed you," he said.

We had been in touch by phone over the months, but our conversations were strained.

He took my hand and led me to the basement without saying anything. He opened the door to one of the rooms that had served as a bedroom for one of the carpenters, turned on the lights, and as my eyes adjusted, I saw a lovely room with the walls painted light blue. Clean, stained birch shelving covered one whole wall—built-in bookcases from floor to ceiling! A tweed grey-blue carpet lay on what had been just a cement floor. A new roll-top desk and comfortable-looking office chair were positioned in one corner, and beside the computer was a vase filled with the large white blossoms of our own hydrangea bush.

"Here's your writing studio," my husband said, as he took one flower out of the vase and handed it to me. "You know I love you." He looked so shy, as if wondering about his skills as an interior decorator.

My eyes filled with tears, and I let myself be gathered into his warm, strong carpenter arms. "I love you too," I said. "And I've missed you so much."

Of course, the sun didn't shine every day after that, and fireworks didn't go off every evening. I filled up the bookshelves in no time. We had a lot of talks and started to figure out how we could both have our retirement dreams met, and then we talked some more.

After the hydrangea blossoms dried, I kept them on my desk so I could remember their beauty and the love they represented. And I'm writing.

—Mary E. Winter

Diving for Love

Thirty years ago when David and I took off for our honeymoon to Hawaii, we carried a lot of baggage. We took just a few suitcases with some light clothing, bathing suits, and sunscreen, but we had plenty of emotional baggage. It was the second marriage for both of us. We'd fallen madly in love a few years before, spent a year in passionate romantic bliss, then a year arguing just as passionately to work out the kinks, and after six months of living together amicably, we were ready to get married.

Three days before the wedding, David brought me to his lawyer's office to sign a prenuptial agreement. Because his first marriage had lasted only a few years, he wanted to be sure, in case ours failed, that he'd keep the house he now owned. I was crushed. Didn't he have faith in our love? But something in me told me to go ahead with the wedding on blind faith. The ceremony was beautiful, the wedding a dream, but on the airplane heading for Hawaii the next morning, I was fighting off tears.

When we stepped off the plane in Kauai, the warm breeze was so playful and erotic that I put aside the baggage and inhaled. Then exhaled, softer. *Yes.* That afternoon we wandered on a beach where hot water gushed up from crevices, bursting every few minutes like warm body fluids. David picked a blood-red flower and braided it into my hair. We had landed in the land of hot love; no broken hearts allowed. The rhythm of the islands enveloped us like new, sweet skin.

In the next days, we danced in yellow moonlight, crooned with ukuleles, sucked on mangos, made slow love, snorkeled on red reefs, and swam with purple fishes. On the fifth day, we decided to venture deeper into the ocean. Instead of spending months getting certified to scuba dive, tourists in Hawaii can take a two-hour group lesson and then dive thirty feet below the ocean's surface with instructors. We were island adventurers, drenched in warm passion and smothered in fragrant leis, so we signed up to swim into the underworld.

The first hour of instruction included a comprehensive list of every possible death under the sea. The second hour squeaked with rubber suits, breathing apparatus, and stark fear. In the heavy wetsuit, my loose, hula-dancing body became stiff and awkward. My swim fins slapped hard on the training deck, jutting out at sharp angles when I tried to walk. The metal tank strapped to my back was leaden, and the flimsy mouth tube my only lifeline. *Place the rubber nozzle in your mouth and breathe slowly. Do not inhale sharply. In and out slowly, naturally.* I envisioned myself at the bottom of the ocean, unable to breathe, the tube floating out of my reach. *Place the mask over your eyes and push firmly to seal. If your vision clouds, tip your head back slightly, and push the seal up and down to let excess water escape.* I imagined my vision clouding as the water rushed into my lungs, my arms flailing, eyes bulging, as I watched one last purple fish float by.

David was grinning as he pulled the apparatus in and out of his mouth, walking easy, tall and lanky in his slick wetsuit—Lloyd Bridges ready for *Sea Hunt.* I breathed into my air hose, *shlshhshhlsh,* and out, *phshhshshhh,* peering closely at the gauge on my tank. *When your gauge goes down to less than one hundred, wave your arms at an instructor. The person whose gauge goes down to one hundred first must signal immediately, and we will all return to the surface. Breathe in slowly, shlshhshhls, breathe out calmly, phshhshshhh.* I began to shiver uncontrollably.

David slipped off his mask and walked closer. "What's the matter?"

"I'm terrified." The shivers had become spasms; my knees were buckling.

"I thought you wanted to do this." David put his arms around me to steady me, reached behind and loosened my mask, then pulled me over to sit on a bench. "Wasn't this your idea, honey?" He was peering at me curiously, as if he'd never met this quivering creature.

"Yes, I do want to do it. I just forgot that I get terrified if I can't breathe."

"Since when?"

"Since this scuba diving lesson."

"Should we forget it, and do something else?"

"No. After all the time to put on this stuff, I want to at least enjoy the view under the water.

A few minutes later I steeled myself as we plunged into the water. My eyes glared frozen from behind my mask, while bubbles drifted up with each breath: in *shlshlshsh*, out *phshshshsh*, bubble, bubble; in *shlshlshh*, out *phsshshsh*, bubble, bubble. I tried to swim, but I couldn't get my legs to unfurl and my arms flapped at my sides, like turtle fins. The instructor floated by me, gesturing. She pointed to my curled knees, then to her own legs, which she waved in an exaggerated mermaid swish. I tried a swish or two, but then snapped back to fetal position. Breathe in *shslshshlsh*, breathe out, *pshshhshsh*, bubble, bubble.

David was somewhere in the drift of divers float-ing in strange, ghostly bubbles. I searched for his face behind the masks, but my own mask was beginning to get cloudy. *If your vision clouds, tip your head back slightly, and push the seal up and down to let excess water escape.* I tipped my head back, then pushed the seal up and down as carefully as I could. When the mask filled with saltwater, I panicked. Though I waved my arms wildly to get an instructor's atten-tion, no one came, so I headed for the surface, alone. *Push up, breathe in,* shlshhshshh, *push harder, kick, breathe out,* phshshshsh, *reach up, splash out.*

When I surfaced, I pulled the mask off my face and blinked. With one hand I rubbed my eyes while my other hand let go of the mask, which drifted slowly to the bottom as I tread water to stay afloat. The shore looked a long way off.

An instructor splashed up next to me. "What's going on?"

"My mask was filling with water and I couldn't clear it." My voice sounded hollow and gurgly, as if filled with bubbles and salt.

"Where is your mask?"

"I think I dropped it."

She nodded, and for a long time we tread water.

"Okay," she said, "I'll go down for it. You stay right here."

You can think about a lot of things when you're treading water in the middle of the ocean, like how far away the dock is, and whether your mask will ever be found, and how long you can tread water, and whether a shark could bite your legs off, and whether a fish could carry your mask home to his fish family, and where is your husband, and what could he be thinking when he doesn't see you on the bottom of the ocean?

The instructor burst up, waving the mask above her head. She helped me seal it carefully around my face. "Don't wiggle it. Just leave it on," she warned. Then she took my hand and led me firmly back underwater.

In the eerie slanted sunlight I made out David's long, thin shape apart from the other divers. He looked lost, darting around, swimming in half-circles. When he saw us coming, he swam up, his eyes bulging behind his mask. The instructor pointed to my hand, then to David's, and placed my hand carefully in his. She pointed to both our hands, then clasped her own hands together and waved them in front of David's face. *Hold on to her.*

David nodded and signaled thumbs-up with his free hand. He would not let go. He held my hand so firmly, in fact, that I let my legs uncurl just a little, trying a mermaid swish here and there, swimming next to him, holding on. David pointed to his chest, then his air hose, and back to me. He breathed in, *shlshlshsh*, and I matched his breathing, then out, slowly, *pshshshsh*; we breathed together. He nodded and we swam off, a two-headed mermaid, breathing in rhythm.

David pointed out a neon parrotfish, then he led me to a little cave and showed me a glowing eel under a rock. *Breathe in together, breathe out together. Swish fins.* It was kind of glorious deep under the sea.

When we emerged, the light was fading but the air was still warm and fragrant. After peeling off our wetsuits, we sat on a bench, leaning into each other, grinning.

The instructor walked over to check on me. "Diving is scarier for women," she said. I looked puzzled. "Because we bear children," she explained.

Rachel was born nine months and three days later. Five months into the pregnancy, when I felt her kicking inside me, I sat David down and placed his hand on my stomach. We sat in silence for a few moments, just the three of us.

Finally I said, "I'm having our child and I need you to put my name on the deed to our home."

Two days later a new deed was issued, and the prenuptial agreement was torn up.

Ari, our son, came three years after.

Now, thirty years and one grandchild later, David and I swim along, drift apart, surface, then dive deeper. We're still holding hands.

—*Debra Gordon Zaslow*

Biscuits and Olives

It was Greg's idea to spend our thirteenth wedding anniversary on Queen Anne Hill in Seattle, just thirty minutes west of our home in the suburbs. I was living on Queen Anne when we met, and years before that Greg had lived there as a college student. He thought it would be romantic to visit the place where we began, the place we'd both left behind.

We stayed at the Marqueen Hotel, a turn-of-the-twentieth-century brick building at the bottom of the hill that had housed apartments for most of its life. The Marqueen isn't plush and new like the tiny boutique hotels downtown; it's large and old-world homey, furnished with vintage décor and antique furniture. If the water ran from hot to cold and back again without any notice, we were willing to trade that inconvenience for a slice of the character we had both loved when we were younger, before the promises of greater safety, bigger back yards, and better schools for our children lured us to the suburbs.

We did everything we wanted that weekend, things we'd all but given up since becoming parents. We ate each meal at a different restaurant, ordering exotic dishes of pheasant eggs and lemongrass soup, curried mussels and dilled crab cakes. We hopped from bar to bar, drinking too many Lemon Drops and dancing to techno-retro music, convincing ourselves that the dark lighting and our penchant for dressing young kept the other dancers from noticing that we were "too old." We spent an afternoon at Pike Place Market, where we felt, almost, like tourists. We bought used books at Twice Sold Tales, which we read while lounging naked in our room until desire drew us away from the pages and into each other's arms.

"Do you miss it?" Greg asked at one point.

I knew he was talking about more than just the neighborhood and city, that he was really asking whether I missed being young and childless and unfettered, with all of my choices still in front of me.

"It's a good question," I said. "Do you have a lifetime?"

"As a matter of fact," he laughed, "I do."

After we had our fill of downtown, we went up the hill—to Kerry Park, for its famous view that spans from downtown to Alki Point, and to the

Queen Anne Café, a diner we used to lounge in over long Sunday breakfasts. Our last stop was the back stoop of my old apartment building, where, fifteen years before, we had shared our first kiss, after hours of soul-meeting talk about music and books and philosophy, important things that would come to seem like mere luxuries in the busy years ahead.

At home after our weekend away, we agreed it was the best anniversary trip we'd ever taken.

But over the next several weeks, as the perfect parts of our getaway started blending into one big happy memory, there was one piece that wouldn't quite mix in. I couldn't help but worry it, turning it over and over in my mind and catching my breath at its sharp edges.

On the last morning, while waiting for the barista at the hotel's coffee shop to steam up our orange-chocolately espresso drinks, Greg picked out a small cookie from a bowl on the counter and put it in his mouth. Just as he was curling up his nose at the taste, a quietly smug voice behind us said, "You just ate a dog biscuit."

We turned then to see a cute, twenty-something girl wearing Northwest-casual city chic, impossibly short hair, and what looked to me like a smooth-skinned face of disdain. We weren't hip enough to know that this café always put out biscuits for its canine clientele (even if they were shaped—

humanly, I thought—like hearts); Greg wasn't cool enough to keep his hands and mouth to himself.

Back at our table, I fumed. "They could at least have a sign," I hissed, embarrassed for Greg—and for myself.

I felt betrayed—by my old neighborhood and its new residents, by my used-to-belong younger self and the older woman I suddenly seemed to be turning into. But Greg didn't care and tried to tease me out of it. He reminded me of how he'd jumped out of a rented car on our honeymoon in Spain to pop an uncured olive into his mouth, only to be knocked to his knees by its brininess. He reminded me of how we'd laughed later, over tapas and beer, and made up newspaper headlines and obituaries: "No looking back: Man, just married, turns into pillar of salt."

I knew I was being silly about the dog biscuit, and I laughed with him, at us. But at home now, I can't quite let it go. I think about all of the girls I used to be: the mysterious one who dressed in black; the manic one who rocketed from job to job and boyfriend to boyfriend, and in between times spent solitary weeks in her apartment, trying to write; the ambivalent one who didn't know if she wanted to marry or live alone, to take the well-paying technical-writing jobs or the poorly paying artsy ones; the girl who was that disdainful young woman in the coffee shop.

The girl I was would never unthinkingly pop something into her mouth, and she certainly wouldn't race to a tree, in any country, as if expecting to taste from The Tree of Life. That girl didn't know that she wouldn't be young forever, that she would be replaced by endless rounds of younger, seemingly cooler girls, all of whom, sooner or later, would also have to choose—between a rooted, microscopic love that could hold her and the telescopic thrill of everything still hovering on the horizon.

I think about how my husband picked me all those years ago, popping me into his heart before he knew what he was getting. How even now that he knows—my bitter parts, my sharp points—he's never once asked for relief, never once shown any regret.

Snuggled into Greg's heart like the pit of an olive, I've accompanied him places I wouldn't go on my own. Sometimes these journeys drain me, as if I've survived too long on dry, tasteless biscuits. But together we've found that even the most unpalatable parts of our personalities, when shared over cup after cup of the creamed coffee we both love, sustain and ultimately strengthen us.

—Lorri McDole

This story was first published in *The Rambler*, October 2007.

Dancing with My Husband

They didn't show this part on *Dancing with the Stars*, I thought, my right foot colliding with my husband's left shin as we attempted to waltz across the dance floor. We tried again, a mixture of love and hysteria in our eyes as I fought hard not to lead and he fought hard not to let me. He had donned the dance shoes he'd worn at our wedding a decade ago, while my feet were dressed in my best Jazzercise sneakers, no high heels to trip me up on this first night of my fantasy-come-true ballroom dance class.

"One, two, three. One, two, three . . ." I counted, loud enough for the two of us as we hurried to catch up to the other two stumbling couples.

There were no cheering crowds to spur us on, no celebrity judges, only fluorescent lights and a sweaty heaviness in the air left over from the hip-hop teens who had occupied the space before us. Kayla, our instructor, clapped her hands and shouted the count from the sideline, looking too young and skinny for us to be friends. No, there'd been no scrolling feed on TV to warn "don't try this at home" or "don't bribe the one you love with tacos and sex every night (not necessarily in that order) for a Friday night dance class," because, hey, now that we're married, we're not doing anything after *Jeopardy*, anyway.

My husband and I finally managed a safe step, two, three, and my heart swelled as Frank Sinatra sang and we glided a few feet across the hardwood floor. I engaged the fantasy, imagining myself in a skin-tight backless dress, the music loud and strong, stirring that falling-in-love feeling when joy courses through you like a low-grade fever. No matter that the last time my husband and I had danced together was at our wedding long ago. No matter that those TV dancers didn't have to race home from work to grab the spouse who'd just arrived from his own nine-to-fiver and dash down to the dance "institute," a converted suite of rooms with mirrors for walls in the token industrial section of suburbia. No matter any of that, because we were here, really here, and for a few more cautious steps I was living the dream. I smiled at my husband, he smiled back, and then, happy and distracted, we promptly ran into each other again.

"Okay, kids," Kayla called. "Gather 'round, please, so I can show you the next move."

She grabbed my husband's hand and pulled him into the middle of our small circle. I watched, helpless, as she bent his arms into position like a life-sized Gumby doll and then locked her frame into his.

"Now, pay attention," she said. "This is what it should look like."

Kayla nodded a silent count to my spouse, then boldly stepped back, pulling my better half with her. I braced, waiting for the crash.

"You're so lucky," said the woman next to me. "My husband wouldn't be caught dead here."

"There was bribery involved." What, I would not say.

She shook her head. "Nothing would get Barry down here. He likes to bowl, but that's about it."

By now Kayla and my man had danced several yards without mishap. If there was any hesitation on his part, it was quickly quelled by Ms. Skinny Tush.

"He's pretty good, actually," my new friend said. "I'm Harriett, by the way."

"I'm Barbara, and that's Michael," I said, turning to offer her a quick smile, but was surprised to see her watching my guy with open admiration.

Curious, I followed her gaze and that's when it happened: through Harriett's eyes, I saw my husband in a way I hadn't since when we were first dating and every inch of him was fascinating to me and all I desired. Before our dance class, he'd thrown on a white shirt and black slacks, and now I stood transfixed by the contrast of his tan hands against the crisp white cuffs—it was so Antonio Banderas-ish. Had he been wearing that all evening?

The music stopped, and Kayla brought him over. "He's all yours!" she said, giving me his hand. I took it.

"Teacher's pet," I teased.

Michael laughed and pulled me close. "The sacrifices I make."

"And I appreciate it." I tilted my head up like Meg Ryan from *When Harry Met Sally*—when she had good hair.

We started practicing again, our moves to Frank's tunes a little smoother now after Kayla's private lesson. I told him about Harriett. "But she doesn't know you're only here for the promise of food and canoodling."

He looked indignant. "Not true."

"What do you mean?" I felt his guiding right hand, warm and familiar, burrow its way to my bare back, T-shirt be damned.

"I'm here," he said, bending slightly to touch his nose to mine, "because you wanted me to be."

Shocked, I pulled away. "Really?"

Michael reached out, and in a roguish, Harlequin romance-type move brought me up against him and whispered in my ear, "Really."

But he already had me at "you wanted me to be." In that Disney moment, I saw all the little things he does: the spiders he's slain, the schmaltzy love notes left where I'll find them (on my pillow, in my purse, taped on the package of the freeze-dried tortellini I planned to resuscitate for dinner), his gentleman's arm on stairs that seem steeper after age forty. But most of all, letting me drag him to a ballroom dance class for the next six Friday nights when he could be home watching *Dirty Jobs* on DIRECTV. I wanted him. I wanted him now.

"Ready?" he asked, setting us into start-waltz position again.

I nodded. "You can lead."

We danced some more, Sinatra wound down, and Michael spun me around into a death-defying dip that made me cry out with laughter. After class, I threaded my arm through his.

"So what do you say next week I ditch the sneaks for a pair of sexy black pumps?"

He grinned. "And nothing else?"

Men. "Uh—no," I replied, then added, "But later tonight . . . "

—*Barbara Neal Varma*

Popcorn Proposal

The room was dimly lit with candlelight and the glow from the fireplace. The crackling sounds of the wood burning coupled with the soft strains of acoustic Spanish guitar coming from the stereo made the perfect duet, setting the mood. On the floor was a red-and-white-checkered blanket with a picnic basket next to it. The crystal champagne glasses on the fireplace hearth were my clue champagne was lurking somewhere near that basket.

I turned to look at Ryan, who simply smiled at me while he lifted the lid to the basket. Inside, I saw cheese, fruit, chocolate, and other treats.

That was the scene that greeted me when I walked in the door from running an errand—an errand I suddenly realized he had contrived to get me out of the house. I had been expecting the noise and confusion that usually greeted me when I walked in the door. Instead of the barking dog, the attacking cat, and the children screaming about who did what to whom and vying for my attention, the house was quiet, devoid of kids and pets, calm and clean. My living room was never clean.

Ryan's beckoning eyes beseeched me to come and sit by him as he patted the spot on the blanket next to him. I obeyed—greedily, happily—and sank into his arms beside him on the floor. He poured two glasses of champagne, one of which I sipped eagerly. Accustomed to fruit punch and milk, I savored this rare treat.

We toasted, sipped some more champagne, and then he took my glass. Like in the movies, he moved closer to me, put his arms around me, and gently lowered me onto the floor, wrapped up in his embrace.

Two hours later, I woke up, cozy and comfortable, still lying on the floor, with Ryan hovering over me, a smirk on his face, watching me sleep.

"You snore," he said, laughter tinting the words and his eyes crinkling at the sides. I love when his eyes smile.

I was mortified. I could not believe that after he'd gone to so much trouble—finding a way to get rid of the kids, planning the entire evening to picture perfection—I had fallen asleep on him!

I suppose that was the moment when I realized, *This guy must really love me.*

And so he does.

That night my children from a previous relationship, whom Ryan had come to love and care for, had gone, on his dime, to a double feature at the drive-in. Inside the picnic basket was a small velvet box, sapphire blue, and inside that box was a gorgeous triad-diamond engagement ring. It was stunning, absolutely perfect.

Once I woke fully, Ryan bent to his knee, took the box, and properly proposed. At that precise moment, before I gave him an answer, my children came bursting through the door, all eager to tell me about the movie and their exciting evening out. The dog, who had been securely relegated to the bedroom that evening, heard them and began barking her head off. My son accidentally kicked over the champagne flute that was on the floor. We rushed to pick things up and get them out of the line of fire.

"This is what you want to marry into?" I asked, only half kidding.

His eyes twinkled and crinkled again. "More than you can possibly know."

By then, the kids were arguing over who was going to take the leftover bucket of popcorn into their bedroom, oblivious to us mumbling together on the floor.

"You're crazy," I said under my breath, while the dog finally broke free from the bedroom and came in to fight for her share of the popcorn.

"About you," Ryan said.

"Are you going to give me my ring?" I asked, while out of the corner of my eye I saw popcorn fly everywhere.

And so he did.

While you might not consider that to be the most romantic proposal of all time—given my napping, its premature ending, and all the commotion that ensued—it remains one of the most, if not *the* most, romantic nights of my life. Romance, I discovered, isn't in perfection. It's in knowing someone loves you enough to stand next to you in the imperfection of real life and smile when plans change and things go wrong. In that moment I realized that if this guy can handle the destruction of his perfect marriage proposal—with laughter, no less—chances are he might actually stick around through some of the tough stuff.

And so he has.

Actually, that wasn't the first time he'd proposed. He had asked me to marry him twice before. I hadn't said no the previous two times because I didn't love him. I did love him; I was certain of that. But I was having a hard time reconciling that inside myself. I'd been in relationships before where I had loved deeply, passionately. Unfortunately, I'd learned early on that love was not enough, that circumstances and differences could overshadow love. In each of those earlier relationships, I'd desperately wanted to believe that love would be enough, but in the end, I was always left with a lot of love and nothing tangible I could hold on to, nothing safe and secure to build a foundation or future upon.

When Ryan first approached me with a proposition of marriage, it was very businesslike. He had good insurance, a good job, financial security. I was broke, had health problems, and was floundering. Our life situations were too disparate; I feared that instead of him lifting me up, I would bring him down. Too many times I'd seen this happen, both in my own life and in others. So I refused his proposal.

Though I wouldn't have admitted it then, I was a little turned off at the lack of romance in his first proposal. Never mind that I had already set the tone by making sure he knew my mantra: love wasn't enough. In retrospect, I realize he was only trying to accommodate me and my beliefs, to give me more than just the love. When that didn't work, he took a different tack.

His second proposal came spontaneously after an intimate moment. He turned to me and said, "See, we're good together. You ought to marry me. Say yes. I've got the ring in my jacket, right over there. Come on. You know you want to."

It made me laugh. But Ryan was serious, and when I stopped laughing, he asked me to marry him more officially. I wanted to leave him with hope, because I did love him very much. Instead of simply saying no, I told him I wasn't ready yet. He told me the ring would be in his pocket, because he knew I'd be ready soon. I was glad he wasn't ready to give up on me yet.

I felt bad for him. Love shouldn't be so hard. He shouldn't have had to work so hard to win me over.

But he did.

After Ryan proposed to me the third time, on a picnic blanket on the floor of my living room, it all came together: Yes, I was right, love wasn't enough. But love mixed with a willingness to work at it, to keep trying against all odds and hope—is that what it takes to have a happy, lasting marriage? Is that enough?

That night, I figured that if the man was willing to work that hard to win me over, he'd be even more willing to work hard to keep me. If Ryan was willing to see past naps during marriage proposals, spilled champagne, and popcorn arguments on the most romantic night of our lives, I figured there wasn't too much that would faze him. I also knew I was ready to make that same effort for him and for us, to make that same commitment to him.

After the popcorn was cleaned up, the kids were tucked into bed, and the dog was satiated on the cheese she managed to steal from the picnic basket while we dealt with the popcorn, I told him I would marry him on one condition.

"I've already promised to love you forever," he said.

"And I'm glad for that," I replied. "But that's not what I'm asking."

He laughed when I told him I would marry him if he promised he would always laugh at spilled popcorn and continue to smile when I snored.

And so he has.

Of course, he recently purchased a heavy-duty vacuum cleaner and some state-of-the-art headphones, but I'm sure that doesn't mean anything.

—*Michelle L. Devon*

How the Funny Papers Rocked My World

Years ago, when Ron and I had been dating several months and February neared, I gently mentioned Valentine's Day. He seemed rather foggy on the topic, so I offered him some assistance. "Shall we have a romantic evening together?" I asked. Of course, what I really meant was, Would you like to surprise me with a romantic evening? But I didn't know him well enough to be that bold.

We both wrote the date on our calendars. We planned to meet at Ron's house and then go to dinner.

I showed up with a gift and card for him inside my satchel, wondering if he remembered I liked daisies better than roses. I was curious about which restaurant he had selected for our romantic candlelight dinner.

"So how about a quick bite of sushi and a movie?" Ron asked, as I was wondering where he had hidden my flowers.

There are not many vegetarians who rate a sushi joint as one of their top romantic venues, but I figured Ron had something eclectic in mind. So I said, "Okaaay," in a slow quiet way that might have warned the astute listener I was less than pleased. Still, I hoped a delightful surprise was nestled inside this rather mundane invitation.

At the restaurant, Ron did not notice my quietness. I knew he liked to save the best for last, so I decided to see what happened at the movie.

Nothing. Absolutely nothing. He was so engrossed in the film that he didn't even hold my hand or put his arm around me. I bit my lip to keep from dissolving into disappointment.

"Do you know what day it is?" I asked Ron finally, as we walked into his house.

"Thursday," he said, confidently.

With that answer, the tears I had been holding in flowed out. "It's Valentine's Day," I sobbed. "We were supposed to have a romantic evening."

"Why didn't you say something?" he asked.

"I did."

"When?"

"Three weeks ago."

"Why didn't you remind me?" He looked sweet and concerned.

I could see he was not a thoughtless, rotten cad, but merely an untrained innocent who had not been educated in the niceties of this holiday. I gave him his gift and his card, then I went home and finished my cry.

For the next couple of years, I gently mentioned the holiday to Ron in advance, suggesting things we might enjoy doing. We made our plans and enjoyed ourselves. But part of me still wanted to be surprised by romance on that one day.

Then Ron added "Cathy" to the comics he read daily. And Cathy added her boyfriend, then husband, Irving. Irving, like Ron, was clueless about Valentine's Day. Unlike me, Cathy minced no words in voicing her expectations and giving out instructions on romance and other topics.

"I am learning a lot from Cathy," Ron said last January.

I nodded and figured he was learning what you say to a woman who has just tried on a zillion bathing suits and bought none. Cathy was great at that sort of gender-based advice.

Meanwhile, I let go of my expectations. I loved Ron; he loved me. I didn't even mention Valentine's Day. I knew we would spend that evening together and it would be enough for me.

"Honey, can you be available on the afternoon of February fourteenth?" Ron asked a week before the day.

"Yes," I said. I had left my schedule flexible, just in case.

"Can you be available on the morning of February fifteenth?" Ron asked.

"What did you have in mind?"

"It's a surprise," he said.

On February thirteenth, he said, "You'll need to pack a suitcase."

I packed a suitcase and was filled with anticipation as we got into the car on the afternoon of February fourteenth. After some driving around, Ron pulled up at a hotel that was unusually elegant for us.

He had everything planned out, including champagne, a romantic dinner, and a stunning view of the city—all without having to go outside in the cold.

"Ron, how did you ever figure out such a delightful getaway?" I asked, as we sipped champagne late that night and watched the city lights.

"From reading 'Cathy,'" he said. "She helped me figure out what you meant by a romantic evening."

And so the comics enriched my relationship. Ron had done all the work, and I had merely let go and let Cathy.

—*Deborah Shouse*

180 Seconds to a Lifetime

"Why are we here?" my friend Pam asked. We looked around the unfamiliar restaurant where we were waiting in line to attend a three-minute dating event in a closed-off room next to the bar.

"It'll be fine," I assured her. "We'll meet guys our age who actually want to date, and we'll weed through them fast."

"So, Miss Queen of Small Talk," she quipped, "where do I start?"

"You could describe your underwear."

A much younger, overdressed man was listening in and smiling too big. When our eyes met, he threw out his hand and introduced himself as Mark, not even pretending he hadn't heard me.

Oh, Doogie, I thought to myself, *I was teaching high school your freshman year.* "Hi, Mark," I said, then lowered my voice to conspiratorial whisper. "I'm just kidding; we're not wearing any underwear."

Modest Pam almost choked on the beer she'd just gulped. But she smiled, ready to play along with any joke.

Mark's grin grew as he took Pam's whole arm in his two hands. "I'm Mark," he said, seeking a hand to shake.

Before Pam could answer or remove her arm, a tall man with unruly hair leaned into us.

"We're early?" he asked, sharing garlic. "There're so many men, no?"

We smiled and shrugged, realizing for the first time that we were outnumbered by the male species, at least at this spot in line. Soon men started asking us where we lived and what we did for fun, like they couldn't wait for the whole show to begin.

The man in front of me turned around and asked, "So what do you for a living?"

"I'm a teacher."

"Ooooh, I went to school!"

"What a coincidence," I said before realizing he was not joking and actually took pride in this connection.

I began to fear the night would be more interesting than worthwhile. Then I noticed him: straight, light-colored hair; steel-blue eyes; broad shoulders;

cute; but probably younger than me. Actually, he noticed me first.

"You're from Naperville," he addressed me. "I'm from Bolingbrook." This established us as neighbors.

"I live in Naperville now. I'm from the South Side."

"I'm from the South Side." He dropped this casually, but his eyes caught mine, challenging me.

"Shut up! You're not." Then, returning his serve, I shot back, "Mother McAuley," naming the large all-girls' private high school I'd attended, one easily recognizable to any South Sider.

"I went to Marist." Marist was the boys' equivalent to my alma mater. "What year did you graduate?"

Too many sets of ears had grown too interested in our conversation, so I went mute.

"I graduated in 1986," he volunteered.

"I graduated in 1986!" I said, deciding to focus only on this same-age alum of my "brother school" and to ignore the eavesdroppers.

"You did not!"

We proceeded to drop names, and our pasts started overlapping. As the world shrunk, I noticed his confidence and warm smile.

"John," he offered his hand.

"I'm Gina." His firm grasp made me swoon. Beaming, I felt a sudden heat reddening my face as the line moved us along.

Pam and I found our assigned places at neighboring tables. Each woman sat at her own table, and the men rotated to talk to us, one at a time, for three minutes each. Everyone received a form listing the name and assigned number of each "date." Next to each name was a line for taking notes and the words yes and no. People with matching yes's would receive each other's e-mail addresses from the organizers the following week.

Scoping the room, I spotted John sitting across from his first partner: Ms. 34, a pretty, young blonde. An announcement told us we had fifteen minutes before the three-minute dates officially started. As a man matching my number, 43, approached, I saw John walk toward the bar. I suddenly felt quite thirsty and darted away before Mr. 43 found our table.

"Gina from the South Side," John said and welcomed me with a one-sided hug, which felt really natural considering our new acquaintance.

We joked and spoke briefly about nothing in particular with a man who stood near the bar.

"Say yes to everything," John insisted when I debated passing up the bartender's offer of peanuts. "If it's free, you want it. Yes, wash my sheets! Yes, bring water! Yes, leave the peanuts!"

I laughed, possibly too much, suddenly a school girl with a crush. I felt oddly at home, despite my racing heart and those piercing blue eyes of his, which seemed to look right through me.

His number was 34, which was both our age and the mathematical reciprocal of my own number, 43. We had grown up only six minutes away from each other, had attended mutual proms, and knew many of the same people. We'd lived almost parallel lives. I wondered how many times we could've met before. Was this fate?

The monitor called for the beginning of the three-minute intervals, and we walked to our waiting "dates."

Before I could sit down, Paul 43 asked, "Do you go to church?"

"Yes," I replied honestly, even though I was put off by his opening line.

"Do you go because you believe in God or because you are afraid of going to hell?"

How long can one-hundred-eighty seconds actually last?

Several men I met that evening presented varying degrees of charm, intelligence, and humor. Jason, who indiscreetly picked his nose, had none of these.

"Will you circle yes for me?" he asked. "I've circled yes for you already."

"Oh! I'm flattered."

"Don't be. I've said yes to everybody. I always do. This is my third event."

"Then you must have lots of great dating experiences."

"No, I've never been matched up with anyone. No one has ever said yes to me."

Trying to act surprised, I surreptitiously circled no.

Though this was my first experience with speed dating, three minutes was enough to determine if someone was worth meeting again, just as I'd predicted to Pam. Other un-marketable men I quickly weeded out included a guy whose wedding ring had left a tan line (duh!) and one who objected to every basic question.

I did meet a few dateable guys early into the evening. That helped me to feel more comfortable and confident; after a while, I found myself having fun. Of course, having a good time didn't mean I desired a follow-up of any sort with most of them. Take, for example, one gentleman who introduced himself as a PhD.

"So, Doctor Ned 38, what do you do for fun?"

"I like rollerblading."

"Do you really? I like rollerblading as well."

"Then we should go rollerblading at Navy Pier. Have you ever done that? I love to take all my first dates there."

"Rollerblading on Navy Pier does sound like fun," I said, omitting the "but not with you" that would have finished that sentence most candidly.

When John 34 sat down for our three-minute date, we really clicked.

We'd talked for only a minute when I heard myself telling him, "If you asked me for my phone number, I'd give it to you."

He leaned forward as if to conceal our conversation from others and to seal the deal. "Really?" he breathed.

With my nod came a rush of giddiness, followed by a warm flush of anxiety. *Maybe that was too eager.*

"That's awesome!" he exclaimed, almost shouting.

Relief washed over me. Then a thrill tickled my spine from tailbone to neck.

We each wrote down our phone numbers and slipped them to one another.

"I'd never call you first, especially after just being so bold," I said.

"Of course. I wouldn't expect that," he said. "I *will* call!"

I believed him. But over the course of two decades of dating, I'd been wrong a few times before.

At the break, John 34 came over to Pam and me and said he was getting tired of answering questions.

"Do you know what I really like to do in my free time?" he asked wildly. "Nothing!" It may've been an honest answer, but in a speed-dating marathon it would've marked him as a loser.

He grabbed my hand and said he was ready to go out for a steak dinner. Giggling, my knees buckled with excitement. I declined—but not before noticing how well my hand fit into his. I was enjoying myself too much to leave. I also wondered if he were joking.

The break was over by then, and we all went back to the tables for the second half of the three-minute dates. At the end of the event, I'd circled yes and taken brief notes for eight of the thirty-two men on my score card. Of course, that meant twenty-four un-dateable guys as well.

Afterward, John and his friend asked Pam and me to join them at the bar. We had drinks, talked, and laughed well into the evening, which for John and me seemed to come to an abrupt stop when our friends were ready to call it a night. Walking out together as a group, we said goodbye in the parking lot.

On the drive home, I became lost not only geographically but also in my thoughts about John 34. Maybe I should have found a way to say good night to him alone. Would he call? He would probably call. He certainly would! . . . Wouldn't he?

When I realized I was driving in the wrong direction completely, I started to turn the car around. Just then my cell phone rang. "Hello?" I answered absent-mindedly, failing to check caller ID and forgetting the late hour.

"How am I supposed to leave a charming and adorable message if you answer the phone?"

I recognized his voice immediately. Laughing, I said, "This is my cell. You didn't even give me a chance to get home!"

We talked through the rest of my drive home, and he helped me navigate out of my unfamiliar environs. We continued to talk as we entered our respective homes and got ready for sleep. After climbing into bed, I talked with him for another two hours! We covered sibling rivalry, grammar school, high school, college, best and worst dating experiences, and summed up that we had gotten more attractive as our friends had married themselves off and the dating pool had narrowed.

"So will you go out with me this Saturday?" John asked.

"Why would I?" I teased. "I already know everything about you." Translated, that meant, *I can't wait to spend more time with you!*

For our first date we went rollerblading on Navy Pier, a great idea courtesy of Dr. 38. I wanted to rip off my wrist guard when John reached out to hold my hand, to feel the warmth and texture of his skin. Still, even through the metal and Velcro, I could feel the perfect fit of our hands. My heart beat faster from holding his hand—and from looking into his intense, blue eyes—than from the exercise!

All that seems long ago and far away as I sit across the table from my husband of nearly six years, both of us tired and overwhelmed. Dinner is on the table, and as we eat we talk about the craziness that is our lives, or try to, while our three young sons—four-year-old Martin, three-year-old Joe, and ten-month-old Tim—pick at their food, poke at one another, and interrupt our conversation. Each of our boys has his own set of intensely blue eyes that seem to look right through us—just as their father's did during those 180 seconds that changed our lives.

"Is this what John 34 had in mind?" I ask him.

"No!" he retorts, and we both laugh.

Though we don't say it aloud, we both know it is so much better than either of us could have imagined.

—Gina Farella Howley

A version of this story was first published in *Southland Family Time Magazine*, February 2008.

Girlfriend

There are quiet, comfortable waiting rooms in hospitals. They have soft, clean living room furniture, a door that closes, and a telephone you can call long distance on, for free. It is not your standard waiting room. If you find yourself sitting in one of these rooms, someone you love is dying. It is where you grieve in private.

Last year I found myself sitting in that room while the internal specialist examined my father. She walked into the room and informed me that my father was nearly brain dead. She said she would try to keep his body alive as long as possible, maybe a few hours, so the family could be called in. Then she hugged me.

If the internal specialist hugs you in that room, you know it's the real thing.

My father did not die within a few hours as predicted.

Miles away and unbeknownst to us, the love of his life, Mary, had also taken a turn for the worst. Somehow, Dad knew. He heard her silent call for help and he responded. My father had one last job to do and he was determined to do it.

Mary and my father dated for nearly a decade before they got married. After twenty years of marriage, he still referred to her as his girlfriend. Having survived a failed first marriage, Dad said he knew what a wife felt like and Mary was definitely more like a girlfriend. It always made her blush or smile . . . or swat him on the side of his head.

Having married later in life, they had a few years of work and drudgery but spent most of their married lives retired. They had time to enjoy one another and they took full advantage of it. There was none of this sitting around and knitting business. No! They lived life to the fullest.

They worked together.

They mowed the lawn as a team of two. She wasn't strong enough to start the mower, and he didn't have enough lung power to push it around the yard, so he pulled the cord to start it and she pushed it.

They played together.

Dad tricked Mary, at sixty years of age, into going to her first strip club. Instead of being embarrassed, she thought it was great fun and laughed and clapped along with the rest of the audience. She asked Dad for money so she could tip the dancers.

Mary bought Dad his first pinky ring. It had a shiny sapphire that she thought matched the color and sparkle of his eyes. She introduced him to an Andy Capp style hat and encouraged him to wear it at a rakish angle.

"She likes me when I'm handsome," Dad would boast.

They lived life together.

Soon after they married, they began traveling together. Winters in Florida or Texas and summers at the lake. They drove across Canada just so they could enjoy the view. There were a few stops at friends and relatives, but most of the time was spent on the road or in each other's company.

On one of their road trips it became apparent that Alzheimer's had become an uninvited guest in their home.

They fought, together.

Mary's bright wit began to fade. They researched everything there was to know about the disease, saw every specialist possible, regardless of how far away he was. They tried every drug, experimented with alternative therapies, prayed to any god that would listen. But they never accepted their fate. They fought the good fight.

As Mary's condition became harder to manage, people suggested that Dad put Mary in a home. He refused. He agreed it would be easier, but reminded us all that he had made a vow to love, honor, and cherish this woman of his heart. No matter the difficulties, he meant to keep his word to her, that he would always be there.

He sold their home, and they both moved into an assisted living complex. It was the right move for a while. Dad fought to take care of Mary for as long as he could. The stress of fighting against the downward spiral caused him to have a heart attack. He survived, but was admitted into the hospital and had to stay there for two weeks. Mary was assessed by the staff and it was determined that she could not stay on her own. They moved Mary to the lock-down unit in the Alzheimer's ward.

When Dad emerged from the hospital, the staff encouraged him to leave Mary where she was and to just come for visits—which he did, every day. Most days he arrived with ice cream. He spent much of his time going to the mall to shop for special treats, regardless of her inability to acknowledge the funny card he would read to her or the fuzzy headed ornament he would show her. He still hoped it would make her smile.

"Just because I can't see her smiling on the outside doesn't mean she isn't smiling somewhere else," he would say. "She's still my girlfriend and she likes presents."

Dad was invited to Europe to visit my sister, but he refused. He couldn't leave his girlfriend that long. "She might get lonely and take up with another fella," he joked, but stuck to his no-travel policy.

Dad's second heart attack came as a surprise for us. Perhaps some part of him knew that Mary was beginning to fail and that is what triggered it. Regardless, forty-eight hours after my father was pronounced practically brain dead, he left the hospital, barely alive himself and in a wheelchair, to go find Mary.

The doctors were against it. The nurses were against it.

He didn't care. He said he was going, with or without their permission. His wife was not expected to live through the night, and he was going to be there, full stop. Seeing his determination, they reluctantly gave him a twenty-four hour pass.

Dad went straight to Mary. Not all of his body functions had come fully back on line yet, but he ignored it all and went to her side, took her hand, and in as strong a voice as he could muster, he said, "I'm here, girlfriend." He repeated it again and again. "I'm here, girlfriend. It's all right. I've got you."

My father fought his way back from death's door so he could say good-bye to the love of his life. He had made a promise to take care of her, 'til death do they part. And he did.

He loved his wife with all his heart. He used that heart, the heart of a lion, to fight his way back from the dead so he could fulfill his promise to always be there for her. If he had not fought his way back, they would have died within hours of each other. But each of them would have died alone.

Instead, he saw her through her death, her funeral, and her interment. He hung on until all the important questions could be answered and arrangements made. Then, a few weeks later, my father finished his journey and joined his girlfriend in the ever after.

—*Allison Maher*

Intestinal Fortitude

I'm too bossy. Sometimes I can't stand myself. For instance, the other night my husband and I were at a wedding reception. We stood near a long buffet table spread with a variety of dishes. On the opposite side of the room, across the dance floor, was another banquet spread.

"Let's go over there and see what it is," suggested my husband eagerly.

"It's the same thing," I said.

"How do you know?"

"I can see it."

This was not true. I just didn't feel like hustling through all those folks meandering about and mingling while waiting on the groom and bride to appear and do the traditional first dance. After the dance, the wait staff would let us guests pounce on the shrimp and crab smorgasbord.

I'm a know-it-all. When we first reached the country club, my husband saw everyone else going through the front door and ushered me that way.

I said, "They didn't read the invite carefully because it clearly said the wedding was outdoors. Look!" I pointed from the parking lot to the grassy lawn behind the club. "I see the white chairs and arbor set up in the back. Let's just walk around to that rather than climb the front stairs and have to go through the entire building and out the back door and back down the back staircase."

My husband acquiesced.

As we rounded the corner of the clubhouse, we spotted the groom's parents on the veranda greeting folks who emerged from the club's back door.

"We need to say hello to them," my spouse pointed out.

So we trudged up the steps to say "Hey" and then down the spiral steps to be escorted to our seats.

The white seats were placed closely together, so I had to sit sideways in mine; otherwise, part of me might have lapped over onto the stranger seated next to me. Then I noticed that all the other guests had fanlike programs.

My husband looked around to see where to get them. I had already figured out that they were given to the invitees as they walked through the building en route to the lawn area where we now sat. But I kept mute. Well, it would have helped to have had a program, because the mike was detached from the minister and attached to the machine of the videographer so the service could be recorded. There was only one outlet for the plug, and that was why we attendees were totally oblivious to what was happening at the altar. Occasionally I'd hear something like, "Let's bow our heads." But mostly it was a domino effect as the first rows heard the minister and then the second row monkeyed them, and so on. But when folks chuckled, I had no idea what the joke was about. So it was like watching a silent movie. I guess nowadays it is more important to have the words spoken for posterity's sake than for those listening here and now.

After the ceremony, we promenaded up the stairs again and waited in line for the reception to start. That was a bit awkward for us because the only folks we knew were the groom and his parents. Of course, I can talk to a gatepost, and I believe I did while we waited in line. My husband nabbed a couple of Arnold Palmer iced teas and a couple of crab cakes.

Once the groom and bride finally danced their first dance and a few announcements were made, they opened the floodgates and we were allowed to feast. A huge spread of shrimp, crab claws, sushi, and smoked salmon was piled high on the table near the veranda doors. My husband and I piled our saucers high with seafood.

"Where's the cocktail sauce?" he asked me.

Being the know-it-all *sans pareil* that I am, I scanned around and glimpsed other guests putting little tumblers of a reddish liquid on their plates.

"Oh, it's in these little cups. It's already done for us individually. How cute."

So we scoured the room for seats, found none, and quitted to the dark balcony near the bar. Since we didn't know anyone, I conversed with the bartender, and he's the one who let me in on why the mike didn't work and why I couldn't hear any vows. He had one meager lantern to serve by and was having a time of it, while we munched down on shrimp tails in the dark.

"This sauce is not very good," I said. "No flavor. Needs horseradish."

We made a big mound of debris from our seafood bonanza. The waitress came to collect our plates. I had put tails in the ashtrays even. She picked up our refuse and asked, "Don't you want your shooters?"

"We are drinking wine," I explained.

"Your oyster shooters."

"I didn't see oysters."

"Well, it's hard to see them in the bottom of the glasses." She held up the tiny tumblers.

"What?"

"These are oyster shooters."

I laughed. "I thought they were watered-down cocktail sauce!"

"Okay. I'll take mine," said my spouse.

"You can have mine too," I said.

"I guess we are the Beverly Hillbillies," I joked.

I worried that seafood debris might be in the tumbler my husband tipped up to drain and hoped he wouldn't choke. The waitress took the empty containers and departed.

We sat and stared off.

"I guess we can get more shrimp," I said.

The bartender piped up. "There's a roast beef station, a cheese station, veggies, and pasta on the other side of the banquet room."

My husband arched his eyebrow.

"Thanks. Let's go." I sprung up and grabbed my husband's arm.

As we strolled over to the banquet spread, I said, "I am such a know-it-all. How do you stand me?"

"Intestinal fortitude," he answered.

We got our plates full of other good stuff, and dodging dancers, retreated to our own little tête-à-tête in the dark corner of the veranda.

"It is beautiful out here with the moon," he said.

I agreed. "After we finish eating, can we try dancing?" I asked, poised for rejection.

He usually doesn't like to dance but said yes. So once we'd polished off round two of the feast, we went inside and danced the swing as others did the shag or whatever they did. We had fun.

We gorged on wedding cake, met a few more folks, and then thanked the bride's parents for a wonderful evening and strolled out to the car.

"I'm sorry I'm so bossy," I said to him. "How do you stand it, seriously?"

"I ignore a lot of what you say."

"And here I thought the reason you never listen to me is because you're just preoccupied. Instead, you're actively screening my comments?"

"What did you say?"

"Never mind."

"Okay."

We put down the top on my convertible Sebring and blazed off on a moonlit night, and I found there really was no need for words, no reason to rehash the evening, no instructions to give. Sometimes, it's good to be quiet and not to be center stage, little miss know-it-all, the tour guide. So I lapped in the night air like a dog hanging its head out the window letting the breeze blow back its ears and enjoying the moment. And I didn't yap the whole ride home.

—Erika Hoffman

Café Amoré

Each morning Andrew walks to the bed cradling the mug in both hands so it won't spill. Like the magi offering a gift, he presents my morning coffee with love and reverence.

"Here you go," he says, hovering by the bedside until I take my first sip. "How is it?"

As always, it—and everything else—is fine.

This morning, something in the way he moved the mug toward me reminded me of our early courtship.

"It'll never work between us," I told him as we walked through the mall, hot coffees in hand. I held my hazel-nut latte under his nose and took perverse pleasure as he recoiled from the sweet aroma. "See?"

"That's not coffee! That's dessert." Andrew shoved his extra-burnt Starbucks' French roast at me. "*This* is coffee!"

"It smells like tar," I said. "Why don't you just go outside and lick the pavement?"

Passersby turned to look at the arguing couple. Surely, ours were irreconcilable differences.

"I drink mine with milk," I challenged him.

"Black," he fired back.

Clearly, we weren't each other's type: Aries/Gemini, conservative/liberal, traditionalist/bohemian. Coffee was the tangible evidence of our dissension. But Andrew persuaded me that coffee could be unifying. He phoned to make dates for a cappuccino and a movie or to rendezvous at a café for a chat over java. He punctuated our favorite activities with coffee.

Just as I began to see his point, I left for a year in Australia. He would mail me my favorite blend and send photos of himself drinking his morning "cuppa joe" alone.

When he came to visit, we explored the cafés of Sydney and Melbourne and learned a whole new vocabulary to underscore our counterpoints. He ordered long blacks. I drank flat whites. Black/white: another contrast. But opposites attract, and we got engaged shortly after my return.

Instead of fighting over closet space, we began our marriage negotiating coffee storage. As we unpacked the kitchen in our new home, I opened the appliance garage and began to unload my gadgets. Andrew wanted it for coffee.

"It's called an appliance garage because it holds appliances," I said. "Otherwise, they'd call it a coffee garage."

"I make coffee every day," he said. "How often do you use those things?"

He was right. My food processor and blender were relegated to a cupboard above the fridge. Crisis averted.

Then he discovered we couldn't share the grinder. My nut-brown flavored beans, smooth and rich as vanilla pods, tainted his glistening dark French roast.

"Your hazelnut coffee contaminated my beans," he complained. How he could taste the subtle flavor under the palate-stripping tar he drank was beyond me.

I pulled my old grinder out of storage. His and hers.

And separate coffee systems, too.

A professor of history, Andrew's coffee system parallels his conservative approach to life. Cone-filtered coffee, no modern electronics or warming plates. He counted scoops of ebony beans and ground them to a fine powder. He measured the water in the kettle, and as soon as it reached the boil, he metered out a slow, steady stream, like a scientist.

I, being an easily distracted writer, used a fool-proof Mr. Coffee® pot. Just flick a switch and walk away. If I became engrossed in my work, the hot-plate kept my coffee warm. Andrew said the warmer ruined the taste.

Even though he abhorred my coffee selection and scoffed at Mr. Coffee, he prepared my java with the same ritualistic care he did his own. Did I want hazelnut or raspberry? He stood in attendance, pouring my coffee the minute it was ready. Sometimes he'd find a new flavor and bring home a sample for me to try: butter pecan, Irish cream, mocha.

When I tired of flavored coffees and mentioned lattes, he came home with a stovetop espresso maker. Without being asked, he replaced my fancy flavors with a variety of espresso beans. The cupboard overflowed with new sample packs.

The morning noises have changed with the brewing. As he heats the milk, the beep of the microwave joins the whir of the grinder. The rhythmic thump of the hand-held frother means my coffee is almost ready.

Now, I lie in bed, writing in my journal, scribbling down my unedited thoughts before the demands of the day intrude. Above the scratch of my pen I hear Andrew's footsteps on the stairs. When I take the mug, its warmth loosens my cramped palm. I sniff the aroma and listen to the foam hiss a greeting.

One morning Andrew presented my latte with a towel draped over his arm. "Please accept this with my compliments," he said with mock formality. I dared him to present it this way every morning. And he does with a laugh.

This week a new dimension was added to our morning ritual. Andrew drizzled coffee through the foam to form the rough outline of a heart. Café amoré. The next day a wobbly turkey adorned my latte. "It started out as a star," he explained. Another morning, the face of a kitten, complete with whiskers, peered out at me.

The ritual, like our relationship, is constantly evolving. This morning, as I take my latte with its foamy petroglyph, I realize that despite our opposing views on everything related to coffee, the brew embodies our cooperation and unconditional love.

When I'm done with my morning cuppa joe, I'll head to the kitchen and clean up the scattered grounds and spills. Tidying up isn't Andrew's strong point, but he makes a mighty fine java. I'll put the kettle back in the coffee garage, wash our mugs, and place them side by side in the drying rack to await the next cup of café amoré.

—*Charmian Christie*

Lost and Found

He'd walked this road so many times. On this day, like so many days before, the chilly Alaskan wind tried to dampen his spirit. His dog had always been his companion on these short mind-massaging treks. She busied herself digging in the snow, scratching and scraping enthusiastically, searching for some mysterious doggie treasure. The nearby airport buzzed with the sounds of a Dash 8 readying for takeoff. Everything was as it always had been . . . except for the angel who accompanied him on this walk.

He felt her gloved hand tighten around his as the wind picked up a notch. Turning toward her, he saw the smile that had captivated him from the moment he had seen her several years earlier, waiting tables in a diner across town. She smiled for no reason other than because they were together. He felt the warmth of her gaze, her perfect dark eyes radiating love as the couple turned toward each other, his own gaze matching hers in intensity. He felt the thrill of her mouth on his as they kissed, embracing life and their love for each other, in the middle of that wintery Alaskan street.

He marveled at God's work. Eight years earlier, she had arrived in tiny Kenai, Alaska, from the sprawling city of Bogota, Colombia. She had come with her sister, and through the strange weavings of life, she found herself trapped and alone in the small northern town. But she persevered, finding the strength and faith necessary to cast aside fears and to thrive in a culture completely different from her own.

It was about this time that an alcoholic wreck of a man was released from the pretrial facility at the nearby Wildwood Correctional Facility. His recent divorce and independent lifestyle had collided in a bottle, and with that crash, his spirit finally had been released. That is when he'd met her—in a small diner, where she worked and he'd stopped in for a hot meal . . . where, innocently, naively, they'd exchanged a few kind words and furtive smiles. He later found out that she didn't even remember him from that day. He, on the other hand, would never forget the unbelievably happy lady who would make this pleasant, but otherwise ordinary, dining experience a life-changing event . . . one day, in the unforeseeable future.

They didn't really get to know each other until a few years later, when she worked at a Mexican restaurant close to his home that he frequented often. His drinking days behind him, his social life became dinner out. And his favorite eating establishment became Rosita's, where she usually found a way to be his server. Although circumstances and caution prevented them from getting too close, they became good friends. Many times, she sat and visited with him during short breaks in her shift, an activity the proprietor of the restaurant allowed, noticing a spark between them that neither of them admitted to.

He began traveling, replacing his drinking life with adventure. The culture and history of Latin America captivated him, and as innocent as it seemed at the time, the day she talked him into visiting her home country, Colombia, and Bogota, the city of her youth, they became closer still. He returned from the trip excited to show her pictures of where he'd been and what he'd seen in her homeland. He remembered her taking his hand in hers as she welcomed him back to the restaurant. He brought her a cross from the Salt Cathedral, which she had suggested he visit.

Over the next few years, the two of them saw more of each other. They went on walks on the beach and in the forest. She gave him Spanish lessons. On occasion, he would put his arm around her, but her reaction was tentative and he realized he was crossing a line. Her personal life was a bit of a mystery to him, and he didn't push her for explanations. But he knew she was in some sort of relationship with another man. And he knew that she was not the type of woman to betray the trust of anyone.

Finally, he weakened. Frustrated, he said some things that put her in a complicated spot. Equally frustrated, she told him to back off, to quit creating a love in his mind when friendship was all they had. A barrier grew between them, and they stopped seeing each other. The Spanish lessons ceased, as did the walks.

On a trip to Africa, he met a South African woman. They got along well and kept in touch with each other over the Internet. She decided to come and visit him during the upcoming summer. He had given up on his Colombian angel. It was time to look elsewhere. He was getting older; time was no longer on his side.

After returning from Africa, his Colombian angel contacted him. She wanted to see photographs of his trip. He always wanted to see her. They got together, and as always, her smile and positive nature overwhelmed him. Despite his situation with the lady from South Africa, the two friends began communicating again. One sunny spring day, they went on a short hike in the mountains, and their worlds began to spin. Without so much as a single kiss between them, the sparks that had been held in check for so many years began to fly. A week later, they found themselves in each other's arms. Their hunger for one another finally found satisfaction as their lips met for the first time. For the first time, the passion in their eyes was released as they looked upon each other. They made love.

Then, he shattered his angel's heart. He would never forget that day. A day after making love to the woman he had adored for so long, he would break her heart . . . and his own. The woman from South Africa was coming. She had turned her life upside-down to fly halfway across the world to be with him. He had to give her his best. He sat with the one he loved and told her of his decision to let her go so he could do what he felt in his heart was right. He would never forget the look in those perfect dark eyes as she bravely took his decision and accepted it. He drove away; she resolved to let him go. In her mind, she had taken him for granted, assuming he would always be there for her. Now, she realized she had waited too long to let him know how much she cared. He was gone.

She spent the summer working long hours and crying her lonely nights away in Wasilla, to the north of Kenai. Her former boss at Rosita's, the one who had seen the spark between them so many years ago, had offered her a new job. As it turned out, that job was the thin thread that kept her in Alaska through that summer.

The man spent his summer waiting for his South African lady and questioning himself for the price he had paid for her visit. Illness and visa problems and every conceivable event got in the way of her travel. Finally, in early October, he gave up. She admitted that the trip would not soon occur. He told her to forget it.

God has such a wonderful way about Him. A work-related phone call caught him by surprise, and for the first time in months, he heard the voice of his angel in the receiver: "Wade?"

"Martha?"

Their conversation was short and polite. To him, however, the message was immense. She did not hate him. He had been so sure she would never forgive him that he had given up on finding her. God had returned her to his world.

A week later, while in the same restaurant where they had met, he met another waitress from Bogota. In casual conversation he found out she knew

Martha. A week later, she told him Martha had said "hi." They had found each other again.

He'd walked this road so many times. But now as the dog dug excitedly in the snow bank, as the Dash 8 rumbled nearby, and as the arctic breeze tried in vain to dampen his enthusiasm, he held his angel in his arms. Her perfect dark eyes held his gaze as he swam in the warmth of her touch. Her lips met his, and the thrill of their love danced through his body as he pulled her tightly against him. He pulled away from her kiss and with his hand gently held her beautiful face against his chest.

Closing his eyes, he whispered, "*Gracias, mi amor.*"

The words were meant for her to hear. But they were also meant for God. Love had found its way to a woman from Bogota, Colombia, and a man from Kenai, Alaska. It had rewarded them for their patience, for their honor. They tilted back their heads and smiled warmly at each other. As they gazed lovingly, knowingly, into each other's eyes, surely God smiled, too, at these two lovers who were meant to be, who had finally found the path He meant for them to share.

—*Wade Morgan*

To Love Greatly

"I will never, ever have a decent boyfriend. Never!" Dayna screamed through a waterfall of tears. "And don't you dare tell me I will, Mom. You can't face the truth, but I can. Nobody good will ever want me."

My heart sank. Choking back tears, I said simply, "I'm sorry it didn't work out for you, honey."

What more could I say?

Dayna, my developmentally disabled thirty-nine-year-old daughter, manages serious perceptual and neurological learning disabilities. She attended a special education program all through school. Romance had not worked out for Dayna, ever. She had recovered from severe breakups of long-term relationships before. This was the second time she'd left her low-rent, HUD apartment for disabled persons to make a go with a partner in another region of our state. When the romance failed, her re-entry into the HUD program and setting up house again embarrassed her and drained me financially. Relying on family assistance to get back on her feet now, at almost forty years old, was almost too much for Dayna to endure. Her self-esteem was at its lowest, and she was convinced no one would ever love her.

A few weeks passed, and Dayna, with her characteristic resilience, put herself back into the dating tournament. She used the Internet and local singles magazines, and she went to local church and social groups. We talked on the phone every Monday night to recap the weekend dating events, and I dreaded the summary evaluations, such as:

"He was nice looking but seemed creepy."

"He kept repeating everything I said."

"I loved his thick, curly hair, but his teeth were bad and his clothes weren't clean."

"He is so anxious. I couldn't relax."

Or the very real, but painful for a mother to hear, "He has even more disabilities than I do, Mom."

Or the even more painful, "He ditched me when I went to the bathroom, and I had to pay for both of our burgers and coffees."

Sometimes the dates were more devious:

"It wasn't even his real phone number, Mom. It was a laundry. Why did he do that to me?"

There was a Tim, a Robert, a Paul, a Ben, a Kevin, a Ron, and someone with limited English skills named "Panji." One suitor was as old as her father. The string of first dates kept getting longer. My heart was breaking for Dayna. Maybe she was right, maybe she would live alone all of her life.

Some twists in her dating scene were just plain odd, as in this post-date report:

"Mom, the man from Maine just dumped me from our date, saying I wasn't fat at all. He was really mad because I'm petite and skinny. He called me a liar."

"I don't understand, honey. Did you make a posting saying you are overweight?"

"I don't think so."

"Well, maybe he has some problems and came up with an idea that you are overweight, or maybe he was hoping you would be large. I don't know."

Then, she said sweetly, "I know I'm a good person, and in my posting I said I am more to love."

"More?"

"Yeah, Mom, you know how you always tell me I am more lovable than most people, that I have more love to give and give it largely. All I did was put my contact information in the 'More to Love' section because you're right, I have more love to offer than most people."

Her brother and I didn't know whether to laugh or cry, and we did a little of both. We imagined the man with a preference for large women finding himself face to face with four feet, eleven-inch, ninety-eight pound Dayna and roared.

Then, just over the New Hampshire border, in Peabody, Massachusetts, Brad, age fifty-one, was convinced that his disabilities ruled out his chance of ever forming a healthy relationship with a woman. His heart and spirit had been stomped on so many times. He decided Dayna, this new woman up north, would be his last try. They compared interests and their religious beliefs. They went on picnics and walked on the Maine and New Hampshire beaches.

Her enthusiasm spilled over into our nightly calls:

"Mom, he even told me that he is special education, too, and he can't read well. His spelling is terrible online. But you know what? He can drive."

That was a big deal, because Dayna would never be able to drive, and getting around on buses and making transfers confused and stressed her.

"So, Mom, what do you think?"

"Don't get in his car. Ask him to park in front of the coffeehouse and then take down his license plate number. When you're in the bathroom, call and record it on my voice mail."

"Okay."

"And remember, say good-bye at the coffee house and don't walk home until you see him go down the one-way street out of the city. Then call me again when you get home at eleven."

"I know, Mom. I have school-learning disabilities. I'm not stupid."

My promotion of her self-advocacy was taking root. Still, she was vulnerable in the dating world.

Brad, as it turned out, would be a powerful force for me to reckon with. I had an uneasy feeling that I wouldn't be able to scare him away.

"Brad says it's time to meet you, Mom. He wants to be sure you like him. He thinks if you don't, you might ruin it for us."

Now there's an "it" and an "us?" My heart skipped a beat, and I had to bite my tongue not to confront her. My mantra was, "Go easy, Mother, or she, they, will dig in their heels." Dayna has made more than one disastrous move out of town, rebelling against me and trying to prove loyalty to a boyfriend. I needed to be very careful.

I faked it. "Why wouldn't I like him, honey? He must be nice if he is making you so happy. I just hope he likes me."

That's right: put him on the defensive with the reverse-psychology approach. It's Dayna's poor old mother who needs to be handled gently, and he will have to prove that he is on my side. Take that, you tall, dark heartthrob. I was feeling smug, sure that this latest guy could not outsmart me. I wanted Dayna to be happy, but I also wanted to be sure the guy would be right for her. I held hope that someone with developmental disabilities could be as sweet as she is and that together, with resources and support, they could improve each other's lives. Still, I doubted Brad was the one. Fifty-one and still living with his sister? This guy will never make it.

Brad did drive and produced a license, registration, and proof of insurance with a safe driver price reduction. My preconceived idea of Brad was beginning to crumble. At dinner, he pulled Dayna's chair out, hung up her coat, and cut her steak, which I had always done because she couldn't navigate a knife.

"I'm so glad we got different dinners, sweetie. Now we can taste each other's and share," Brad said happily as he clasped her hand.

They grinned at each other. He ordered her coffee very light, no sugar, iced. She reminded him not to put the salsa on his chicken because it would give him heartburn. He redid the last three bottom buttons on her blouse, which she has misaligned. She read the dessert menu out loud because he is a slow reader. They managed to split their check fairly and asked for my help to figure the tip. They sat close, exchanged knowing, intimate glances at each other, and cuddled. It all seemed so . . . normal. What was happening? They were happy, and it was infectious. I floated to my car.

A few weeks after this dinner, I was visiting Dayna at her apartment when she ran into the kitchen waving her portable phone and asked me to show her how to put it on speaker.

"Mom, Brad wants to talk to you," she said excitedly.

"Hello, Priscilla," Brad's voice was very loud, and he sounded nervous. "Dayna and I have decided to move in together." No icebreaker.

"Brad, there is no way she is giving up that beautiful apartment and moving out of state."

"Oh, I know. She made that clear. I'll have to leave my sister's apartment. That's where I've lived since our mother died, two years ago. I'm not sure what to do because I never moved away from my family."

His mother died? Dayna's father died a year ago. And I have worried more over her future since I became widowed.

"I'm sorry your mother died."

"And I'm sorry your husband died. I help Dayna about her grief over her dad. My mother had cancer, too. We know we can't live with our families all of our lives, because our families die before we do. We have to be our own family, so we can take care of each other. We hope you understand."

There was a strong, well-defined, and purpose-driven "we" now and it brought me more relief than concern. I had to say the right thing. It wasn't about me; it was about them. And I had to give them a fighting chance.

"Brad. Dayna. Of course I understand." Each word had to be pushed out, like a birthing.

Dayna burst out with, "Oh, thank you, Mommy!"

Brad right behind her. "Thanks a lot, Priscilla! We appreciate it."

It was a good start, but they deserved more. No more faking it or manipulation. Brad had grown on me, and I appreciated what he brought to my daughter's life. So I offered, "What can I do to help you two?"

They put in their wish list, and over several months, they moved in as a couple, each named on the HUD lease.

Yes, Brad and Dayna continue to hold their own. They're happier together than they were apart, and they improve each other's lives. That they are disabled is the lesser portion of their identities. Primarily, Brad and Dayna are defined as a happy couple.

To this day, every time I hear either of them say "we," I smile. And my heart leaps when I watch them kiss each other hello or goodbye, always followed by their mantra, "I love you greatly."

—*Priscilla Carr*

Garlic Soup

I stand at the doorway, hands in my pockets, rocking back and forth on my heels, watching him cook. I'm not allowed in the kitchen here, at his mother's house, where he lives. He does all the cooking for her and for me—long, elaborate meals with big pots and many dishes. Years of working as a cook in Spain taught him the value of fresh ingredients, small portions, finesse preparation. He doesn't start with a recipe, but with a feeling. Then he slices and mixes and stirs, sometimes allowing me to stand behind him and watch. But mostly I am banished.

I stand there, needing one last thing from him. Without talking about it, we have slowly made our separations. My books gradually made their way back on my shelves. His CDs had been returned to the rack, one by one. We have divided up the mementos from our two summers in Spain, me giving him most of the coins and postcards to share with his Spanish classes. I took all the maps. We each got a set of pictures. We are running out of property to divide and are inching perilously close to having to talk about our unmaking.

Two years dating, and still no commitment. No "I love you." Not much physical contact. We move through the world like brother and sister. As humanities professors at the same university, we share the same geography, the same general worldview, the same politics. We both love good food, and he cooks garlic soup for me when I am sick, bringing it to me on a bed tray. We both love to travel, and we took two trips to Spain together, my first time outside the United States. We both love to ride bikes, and we have ridden everywhere we can on two continents.

Overall, we are easy together, so we continue on like sixth-grade kids who say they are "going together" but don't really know what that means. Yet, this is no longer working for me. Obviously, it has never truly worked for him either. We are ready to move on, and our most recent experiences in Spain made it all the more clear that we need to.

We're in a bar in Piles, a small pueblo south of Valencia. The friends at our table have a small boy sitting between them. For once, I can keep up with the conversation because everyone is speaking slowly enough so the boy can keep up. Finally, I can participate. I talk more than any other time since I've been in Spain. I start to feel confident.

"Where are you going next?"

"*Extremadura*," I answer, the home of the conquistadors.

Then, as I struggle to find the Spanish words to explain that I am a woman with some American Indian blood, returning to the Old World to follow in the footsteps of the conquistadors, John interrupts me and explains my research in fast Castillano.

The friends look from him to me, pleased and surprised.

"Why are you so interested in the conquistadors?"

"Because . . ." I roll into my answer at a good pace.

John interrupts me to correct my verb tense. Twice. From then on, each time I speak in Spanish, he cuts me off, corrects me, or ignores me. Finally, I quit.

This scene is repeated as we backpack across the country to Extremadura, into Portugal, and back across the border. We visit museums, libraries, and research centers devoted to the conquistadors. We look at faded documents in sixteenth-century Spanish, as different from the Spanish I know as Shakespeare's English is from the language my West

Virginian students speak. John becomes my voice, asking for the answers I need. He also makes meaning for me, translating what I hear, explaining what I see. He loves his role as leader.

At home, in the United States, he is in my territory. Spain is his turf, and he wants me to know it. I can do little without his approval, his help, his control. I had learned in my graduate studies that the language we use shapes our thinking. Now I learn how true that is. I develop such a complex about speaking Spanish that I can't breathe whenever anyone speaks to me. My thoughts become fragmented, and I feel hesitant and confused. I don't initiate conversations. I stop going out on solo adventures. I become fearful of what I can't even name—that something will go wrong, that I won't be able to find my way home. That I will lose him, my link to the world.

We've rented a car to drive back to Madrid, and I see, for the first time, a field of sunflowers stretching as far as I can see. I love sunflowers, with their preposterously large heads that follow the sun's movement across the sky. I love the small yellow petals, like rays from a black star. I also love sunflower seeds, crusted with salt and crisp. I want to walk in the field, to see that abundance stretched before me. I want to touch them.

"Can we stop?"

No answer.

"I'd like to take a picture."

No answer.

"John, please."

"No! No! No!" he finally yells. "Not now, not ever. We're not stopping like tourists along the road to take a stupid picture."

I look at him, dumbfounded.

"You don't get it, do you? Without you, I fit in here. Without you, no one knows I am from the United States. Without you, they all think I am Spanish. You blow it for me. I'm not a tourist, but you make me one."

I turn to watch the sunflowers pass by as the car moves away.

In his mother's kitchen, back home in the United States, I watch him turn the tortilla from the omelet pan onto the plate.

"Can you write down that garlic soup recipe for me?"

He doesn't turn around, but takes a deep breath. He steadies himself with his hands on the counter. He turns and comes to take my hand. "Come here. I'll show you."

I enter the forbidden kitchen. In a dry pan, he tosses the bread cubes to make croutons. He takes down a bulb of garlic, breaks it in half, and we each start to peel. We place the boullion in the warm water to let it dissolve. We slice each clove, tossing the thin pieces into another pan with heated olive oil. When they are transparent but not yet starting to brown, we pour in the pimenton and let the spice warm up in the oil and mix with the garlic. Then we pour in the water with the boullion and stir. Once it boils, we slowly add the beaten egg, letting it dribble in like egg drop soup. We let the egg cook and turn off the heat. We ladle it into a bowl, his hand over mine on the handle, and we sprinkle in the croutons.

John writes down the recipe for me. Then I take my bag of pictures and leave.

Later, as I look through the pictures from Spain, I find one that isn't a photograph. It had been carefully cut out of a magazine and backed with construction paper. Then it had been laminated. The picture shows a field of sunflowers, disappearing into the horizon. His last gift. Apology, forgiveness, acceptance, love. I still have that picture. I keep it to remind me of how love takes many forms and of how, sometimes, it can appear in a final gesture of simply letting go.

—Amy Hudock, PhD

Love Check

As I search through a basket filled with assorted scented soaps, I'm absorbed with selecting a birthday present for a woman friend, my mind far, far from romance. But there beside the basket I find a small, pink book. I pick it up and read the cover. Printed in a dreamy script across overlapping hearts, the title Love Checkbook sounds intriguing. I look inside. The size of a checkbook, this novelty gift contains one hundred pre-printed coupons for one lover to give another, pledging an assortment of mostly PG-rated presents: a walk in the park, a bedtime massage, a no-sports weekend, a romantic dinner, one hundred kisses. Like a bank check, each pink coupon contains a line for the recipient's name and a space at the bottom for the giver's signature. Printed under the signature line are the words "Your Devoted Lover."

Twenty years ago, I would have thought this checkbook interesting but contrived. Two years ago, I would have judged it hopeless. But now I picture an opportunity for my husband and me to walk on the beach, read to each other, or sneak away from the office for a midday rendezvous. The thought occurs to me that I want to do these things with him again. Priced at twelve dollars, the checkbook is worth a try.

When I arrive home, I find our son building Lego racecars and our daughter talking on the phone to a string of friends. My husband, Kirby, sits on our bed reading a magazine and without looking up says, "How was shopping?"

"I found Monika a great gift," I begin, but feel as if I'm talking to an empty room. Pulling the love checkbook from my purse, I toss it onto the bed beside him. "I bought these for you."

Picking up the book, Kirby flips through the pages. I search for any change in his expression, but he looks at the checkbook with less interest than I perceived in his face when he was reading the magazine.

"Thanks," he says. He shifts his weight on the bed so that he can push the book into the back pocket of his jeans. Then he resumes reading.

I had planned to explain that I'd bought the certificates for us to give each other, but now I don't.

What was I thinking? How impractical of me to buy that checkbook!

The next morning, my workday starts earlier than my husband's and kids', and I'm out the door before they wake. My day is completely scheduled, with one meeting after the other, and by midday I have to travel to another city for an afternoon staff meeting. I know the area well, and calculate that I have time enough to stop at the nearby Subway for lunch. It's after one o'clock, and the restaurant is empty.

"Lettuce, tomatoes, and olives," I say to the woman making my sandwich.

A couple walks in, her arm around his waist and his around her neck. They get in line behind me. Only they, the two employees, and I are in the restaurant. As I reach into my purse to pay the cashier for my chicken-breast sandwich, the couple stand next to me at the counter and start to kiss. They kiss once, then again. Their third kiss is prolonged, indiscreet.

I quickly carry my sandwich and Diet Pepsi to my favorite table near the back, but not the last table, and facing the windows. With just twenty minutes before my next meeting, I look forward to being alone. Relaxed for the first time since six o'clock this morning, I concentrate on opening my sandwich and I sip my Pepsi.

Directly behind me, I hear the smacking of lips. I turn to find the couple sitting in the booth nearest me. They kiss loudly. I pause, jarred by their rudeness. Except for my table, they had the whole place to themselves. They keep kissing. Their sandwiches lay tightly wrapped on the tray in front of them. I think of moving and decide instead to ignore them, refocusing on my lunch.

On our first date, twenty-five years ago, Kirby took me to a fish-and-chips place.

"Best fish and chips in town," he said.

He didn't ask me if I liked deep-fried fish topped with catsup and tartar sauce. I didn't, but surviving on a college student's budget, I knew the towering pile of thick French fries and deep-fried cod were a bargain. I found Kirby intelligent and tender. I loved his blue eyes and the fullness of his lower lip; I didn't care about the food.

I turn again to glance at the couple sitting near me. Their eyes are on each other, and they whisper, smile, and touch each other's cheeks. The man looks older than the twenty-something woman, maybe in his late thirties. His face is tanned and rough, as though he works outdoors. Wearing a red T-shirt, she is short and heavy, and her black hair falls into her face. I wonder how they stole this midday moment together. Do they have children? Do they work together? Are they married or having an affair?

I look at the efficient, stark environment: food counter, soda fountain, straight aisles, and hard booths. There are no slim waiters here, no orchids and votive candles on the tables, no dim lights to encourage handholding; yet for this couple, Subway fuels romance.

That evening, after our children are in bed, I find Kirby working at his computer. I hover near him trying to read the screen. *How important is the work he is doing*, I wonder?

"Are you going to be a while?" I ask.

"Another hour or so."

"What are you working on?"

"A report due tomorrow."

I consider waiting that hour for him, but I have my own list of to dos and need to be rested and alert tomorrow. I go to bed wishing that Kirby and my schedules were not so different or that my family lived nearer and could watch our children for a weekend. When we fell in love years before, we couldn't think of anything more lovely than to build a life together. We did. And even though I believed it would never happen to us, we, as a couple, got lost in the very life we made.

The next morning, Kirby and the children leave before I do. After I fit in one more phone call, I can take off for work. Dialing the number and adjusting the pillows on my bed for back support, I'm annoyed with something poking under my shirt. I reach behind and pull it out from under me. It's a pink check with hearts on it. One of the love checks?

I read: "To Patricia: Payment of a romantic dinner for two. —From Kirby." I read it again. In the payment-due section Kirby gave me two weeks to cash in his offer. A deadline? Aren't we both too busy to meet deadlines? I read the coupon a third time. It sounds luxurious, a dinner for two. I remember the couple in Subway and their untouched sandwiches. I write, "ACCEPTED!" in huge blue letters across the coupon and place it on top of Kirby's pillow.

But as I grab my purse, I glimpse the coupon resting on the king-sized pillow, a small, light piece of paper with its edges curled up. I envision it slipping off onto the bed and getting buried in the sheet and blankets, or when Kirby opens our bedroom door, being caught up by a gust of air and floating unnoticed to the floor. If that happened, it could end up lost under the bed. I push the palm of my hand deep into Kirby's pillow, forming an indentation. There in the furrow I nestle the pretty pink invitation for a date with my husband, where he's sure to find it.

—*Patricia Ljutic*

Improv at the Altar

Walking in late to the shipboard commitment ceremony on our women-only cruise of Alaska, my partner Barbara and I took in the scene. At least 100 of the 800 mostly lesbian passengers had gathered for the event. Everyone except us was dressed in fancy clothes; we wore shorts and tees. One by one, a member of each couple said their names, where they lived, and how long they had been together. Those whose relationships spanned more than ten years received hearty applause from everyone—except me. My hands stayed at my side because I never assume that the quantity of a relationship is indicative of its quality. Take, for instance, my parents' highly dysfunctional marriage, which ended just short of their twenty-fourth anniversary with the premature death of my mom. So let's hold the applause unless we know that a couple's long-term relationship is also a good one.

When it was our turn to introduce ourselves, I grabbed the mike and said, "We've been together fourteen years. I was a child bride."

Titters from several of my fellow passengers and a few hearty guffaws greeted my comment.

Silence, though, deflated the good cheer when I added, "I think the quality of a relationship, not its length, should be the measure of its success."

The person leading the ceremony quickly moved on to the next couple, not wanting the event to become memorable for the wrong reasons. Barbara, who insisted on attending the event over my weak objections, shook her head, none too pleased with my comments but not surprised.

A few years before the cruise, we registered in New York City as domestic partners, with no hoopla. No announcements went out to friends and family, and needless to say, we didn't register at Pottery Barn, Saks Fifth Avenue, or L.L.Bean. We certainly had cause to celebrate, having survived some very rough patches, the worst being when Barbara wanted a child and I didn't.

Why didn't we celebrate our domestic partnership? Speaking for myself, I know that the constant battle to educate heterosexual people who trivialize our relationship takes its toll. How many times have I heard myself referred to as Barbara's "friend" by individuals who knew we were a couple? Or had to respond to strangers asking if we are "sisters"?

Internalized homophobia plays a part, too. Never mind that Barbara and I had worn matching silver rings and attended gay rights marches for many years. Never mind that it had been many years since we "came out" to straight friends, relatives, and colleagues. In the middle of the night, thoughts still popped into my mind that because we didn't have the rights of a married couple, our relationship was inferior. If I died before Barbara, for instance, she wouldn't get survivor Social Security benefits, and vice versa. So what was there to celebrate?

These feelings surfaced when Barbara said to me one day, a couple of years after the cruise, "I'd like to have a party to celebrate our twenty years together. How about having it at the Cornelia Street Café?" We both enjoyed having dinner there, and the downstairs room could be rented.

Not wanting to nix the idea outright, I countered with, "What if we took my cousin up on his offer to have a party at his house in Maine?"

When we visited the previous summer, we mentioned our upcoming two-decade anniversary, and he and his wife enthusiastically invited us to celebrate with them. This option appealed to me because I figured only a few adventurous souls, if any, would schlep 400 miles north of New York to party in the middle of nowhere.

"Do you want to have the woman who married us to officiate at your ceremony?" my cousin asked, when we called to discuss details.

"No!" we both immediately answered.

Since we couldn't legally marry in Maine, what was the point? We decided there would be very little conventional about our celebration. No vows, no bridal bouquet toss, no exchange of rings. While the idea of publicly marking our partnership made me nervous, I desperately wanted the invitees' support and good wishes—so much so that I challenged myself to convince as many as possible to spend their July 4 weekend with us up north. I worked the phones and e-mail, coaxing even the most diehard New Yorkers.

Thirty-two friends, some from as far away as Utah, New Mexico, and Hawaii, joined us for what turned into a four-day event. The first night we dined with the early arrivals at a nearby restaurant. The second night we barbecued and karaoked. On the third night, we decided to have some sort of ritual involving, of all things, wedding dresses.

Jeanie, my cousin's wife, had four bridal gowns hanging in a closet that she'd bought for $10 a piece at a consignment shop. She intended to sell them on eBay but hadn't gotten around to it. A formal pink taffeta gown and some Halloween costumes—including a man-size replica of the blue-and-white checkered jumper and puffy white blouse Dorothy wore in *The Wizard of Oz*—also took up space in that closet. I knew I would be wearing one of the wedding gowns because Jeanie said so. If you bring thirty-two friends to someone's house for four days, you'd better agree to almost anything. Barbara, however, adamantly refused to don a gown and dressed up in white pants, a gold cummerbund she had had made for the occasion, and a ruffled white shirt and cufflinks.

Thinking it would be a shame to leave the other gowns in the closet, I asked three female friends—including seventy-five-year-old Jackie, a manly looking woman who hadn't worn a skirt in decades—to play dress up with me. They were more than happy to oblige, quickly getting into costume. Jackie looked positively regal in bridal attire, as it brought out her feminine side, which she literally had kept under wraps since the sixties.

"Next," cousin Jeanie said, as she directed the members of the procession down the stairs and into the sunroom, where whatever was going to happen would take place. Waiting below, the guests whistled and clapped as the three women in bridal gowns majestically descended, trailed by the "flower woman" in the pink gown. Next came me, with a veil doubling as a mosquito net, escorted by cousin

Binky, a bald man in a peach-colored, floor-length cocktail dress, looking like Gandhi or maybe Ben Kingsley playing Gandhi. Unlike the great pacifist, though, Binky chose this moment to bicker with me about why I had set him up on a date fifteen years ago with a friend who was now a lesbian.

"Because she was dating men back then," I kept telling him, close to losing it as we entered the room.

Barbara followed on the arm of her boss, a leaner, taller Sigmund Freud-type, wearing the replica of Dorothy's *Wizard of Oz* costume. Bringing up the rear was cousin Jeanie in a sexy black cocktail dress.

Completely inappropriately, yet oddly apropos, my sister played the syrupy theme from *Love Story* on her saxophone at full blast as we assembled in the sunroom. While poking fun at conventions, the ceremony had touching moments that moved more than one guest to tears amidst all the laughter.

Barbara sang Violeta Parras "Gracias a la Vida," a hymn in praise of life and love that expressed her gratitude for having me in her life. I recited "Love's Passage," by poet Robert Spector, which is full of sea imagery, perfect for a summer evening in Maine, even though we were inland. "Nothing compares with the joy / Of making a landing / In that special harbor / The heart has been heading for"—evoked for me the sense of security I feel with Barbara. I also shared the text of the recent birthday card from Barbara: "The two of us have been through it all—passion and heartbreak, laughter and tears, fighting and making up, ups and downs." The punch line was on the inside: "And that was all since yesterday."

The guests urged us to kiss, which we did, several times. Photos were taken, food from the local Thai restaurant appeared, a friend gave an impromptu mini guitar concert, and the two of us emceed a roast of ourselves equal to a Friars Club affair. Part street theater, part schmaltz, the ceremony and post-ceremony were just the way Barbara and I liked it. Apparently others did, too.

"Central Maine has never seen anything like this before or since," quipped one of my cousin's friends, a local.

Would my partner and I have had such a wacky fun-filled celebration if we had been a straight couple? Most likely not, which is one of the things I like about being a lesbian. Yes, we would like the same legal rights that heterosexual married couples have. But rather than sitting around waiting for that day to come and feeling inferior for what we don't have, we've decided to celebrate milestones as they occur, sprinkling our relationship with affirming occasions like our twentieth anniversary. That's quantity with quality, folks.

—*Michele Forsten*

The Romance of Ordinary Days

I'm in the kitchen chopping celery, dicing onions, quick-frying chicken, and adding broth and finally noodles, for the quintessential cold remedy. When I look out my kitchen window on the thirteenth floor of our condominium building, the exhaust from the shorter building chimneys and houses hangs close to the rooftops. On this Tuesday in February it's so cold that the pigeons are huddled over the hotel roof vents.

Honey's doubled over in his favorite chair. His face is red and perspiring. My heart goes out to him. It's got to hurt to cough so hard.

"Honey, can I get anything for you?"

He's gasping for air. He shakes his head. Waves his hand in the now familiar "I'll be okay" gesture.

I sit on the couch, "Come and sit over here. I'll rub your back."

His eyes are glassy. His brown dressing gown is open and his grey chest hair spirals over the edges.

"The soup will be ready soon. Will you have a small bowl before you go to bed?"

He shakes his head. "Maybe later."

"It'll be ready when you need it. We'll just pop it into the microwave."

When he sits beside me, I hear the rattle in his throat. My hand begins its familiar roam over the dips between his vertebrae and across the smooth muscles and around the moles.

"That feels good. Thanks. I'd kiss you but I have this cold. I don't want to give it to you," he says.

Honey sleeps beside me in our bed and the germs won't recognize the difference between his side and mine, but he has my best interests at heart. I kiss his forehead.

"I'm going to go to bed and read my *History* magazine for a bit," he says.

Going to bed and reading is Honey's signal for a nap even when he's well. I'm not saying that he doesn't read, but it doesn't take long for the magazine to fall to the comforter.

When his mother passed on, we found a few items from Honey's childhood in a trunk. On our entertainment center now are two green metal army tanks and one cannon with a trigger that can still shoot toothpicks at the soldiers standing with rifles raised or lying on bellies aiming at the distant enemy. Sometime during the 1950s, these Dinky Toys appeared in his Christmas stocking. When he and his childhood buddies get together, they always tell stories about the summer when they were nine and curious about the strength of the powder hidden in red paper with a fuse and matches that slid across a rough surface and flared. They blew up miniature Chevy Bel Air convertibles, Ford wood-paneled Country Squire station wagons, and Chrysler Windsor sedans with firecrackers. Honey's few cars that remained char-free were passed on to our sons when they raced along imaginary roads carved into the sand while they visited their grandmother.

This past summer, one son married on the beach against the blue ocean in Waikiki, where we were introduced to the lei tradition, the endless circle of love. The second son will marry next summer with the Canadian prairie sunset as the background.

Today, there are brochures on the counter for a planned cruise to Alaska. Another item on life's bucket list will be completed this September, even though I'm concerned about motion sickness.

"They've got pills for that," Honey says. "Think of the icebergs, the gold rush towns, the plants that survive in that climate, and the people we'll meet. Perhaps we'll see whales."

I'll buy the pills, and we'll share another adventure. During forty years with Honey, I've learned to hug a mountain cliff with my snowmobile, tilted my pelvis during an approach golf swing to the green, and basked in his support while I studied the craft of writing.

Before I go to bed, I spoon four measures of coffee into the filter and fill the water cavity to the seven-cup mark. It's ready for him when he gets up at 5:30 A.M. All he'll have to do is press the "on" button. When I check in on him, his light is out and he's breathing regularly because he's wearing his mask for his CPAP machine. Many years ago, there were nights when I would lie awake counting until he resumed breathing. He didn't realize that he stopped, but when he gulped for air, I relaxed. The snoring that rumbled the rafters was comforting, until once again he became silent. After his diagnosed sleep apnea, the first time Honey put on the gear that would keep his throat open at night, the boys and I laughed at the funny coiled hose and plastic nasal mask that looked like an apparatus out of *Star Wars*. With the laughter out of the way, he slept.

When I snuggle into bed, I put a pillow between us to block the overflow of pressured air from the mask and sleep without counting between his gasps for breath.

It's a dark morning when I get out of bed after him. The welcoming coffee aroma lulls me for a moment, until I notice Honey on the balcony in his robe and slippers, smoking a cigarette. When he steps through the door and he is out of the minus twenty-two degrees Fahrenheit winter, I ask, "How did you sleep?"

"I slept great," he replies.

He sits on the sofa and watches the business channel, switching to the weather channel and over to the local news. He coughs through another spasm, and the sound, I'm sure, breaks the safe decibels for both our ears.

I take two deep breaths. "How's your coffee? Do you need a refill?"

"You have a cup, and if there's some left, I'll have a warm-up."

I'm cautious but I need to ask. "Are you well enough to go to the office today?"

"Yes, I'll go, and if I feel worse, I'll come home early. Why don't you phone a friend and use our tickets to the theater tonight?"

"That's a good idea."

He's handsome in his charcoal suit, crisp white shirt, and blue diamond tie.

"Have you got your Fisherman's Friend lozenges?" I lift his overcoat from the hanger and find his gloves in the basket.

He pats his coat pocket, "Right here."

I see him tap his other pocket, where he keeps his cigarettes and matches.

I step into his arms, and he wraps me tight. His touch, his shape, the smell of his cologne are so much a part of me, of us.

He kisses me quickly. "Sorry about the germs."

"I'd rather have a cold than not have a hug and a kiss."

"You know that I won't always have a cold." He kisses my forehead. "What are you working on today?"

"I'm writing about love."

"Oh, chocolates, unexpected roses, and walks on the beach."

"Yes, but I want my story to be about the love that's there every day, between the bouquets, evening strolls, and dinners for two."

"It sounds like us."

"Yes, it does." I nudge against him.

A small smile plays on his lips. "I'll call you later."

I step away. He has his work to do and I have mine. "Later, honey."

—*Annette M. Bower*

Love, Italian Style

I fell in love when I was eighteen and visiting family in my mother's hometown in Italy.

"Do you remember this young man?" a relative asked me as a motorcycle roared to a stop behind us on the cobblestone road.

I turned around shyly, self-consciously tugging at my miniskirt as the young man took off his helmet and beads of perspiration tickled my chest.

"Yes," my voice cracked as I forced a smile. How could I forget? "Ludovico, right?"

"Sylvia," he said, looking at me intently, his eyes filled with passion. "The last time I saw you, you were ten years old."

And I'd had the hugest crush on you, I wanted to scream, but instead licked my dry lips. "And you were thirteen."

He broke into a dazzling grin, and my heart melted.

I felt his gaze rake over me with silent appreciation, and my body tingled.

"You've changed," he said.

The last time I'd stood before him, I was a gawky child. My appearance had improved somewhat, my body having filled out in the right places, contact lenses replacing my thick glasses, and a bad haircut grown into long, flowing red tresses. I wasn't a supermodel, but I certainly had changed.

"Yes. So have you," I said.

He was just as beautiful as the last time I had seen him, only now his dark features were more refined and mature, his boyish body now muscular and lean. He was gorgeous.

"How long are you staying?" he asked.

"Um, only a few more days."

"Do you want to go for a ride later?"

"Sure." I swallowed nervously. "I'm staying at my aunt's place. Up on the hill?"

"I know where it is."

"I'll be there around five o'clock then?" Ludovico asked.

I nodded.

"Great!" He smiled and put on his helmet. "See you then!"

Five o'clock couldn't come soon enough!

I was very nervous as I waited for Ludovico in the front hall of my aunt's house. Right on time, a motorcycle revved its way up the drive.

"Hello." He smiled as I walked toward him.

"Hi," I breathed.

"Have you ever been on a bike?"

I shook my head no. "I'm a bit nervous." At least that gave me an excuse for my chattering teeth.

"Don't be," he reassured me. "I've been riding for years; you're in good hands."

"Okay," I gulped.

"Let's put this on you."

He gently placed a small helmet over my head, his fingers brushing against my chin as he fastened the clasp. I felt tingles down my spine as his skin touched mine.

"Now, hop on."

I quickly realized that riding on the back of his motorcycle meant sitting quite close to his beautiful form. I tried not to think about how good it felt. *It's only a ride*, I told myself. *He's just being nice.*

Then, before I could think about it any more, we took off like a bolt of lightning—or at least that's how it felt to me—and were zipping along antique streets and weaving up the steepest road I had ever seen in my life. We stopped atop a mountain overlooking the town.

"Wow!" I gasped. "This is so beautiful!"

"Yes." His voice was full of emotion. "Beautiful."

It took a moment for me to register that he wasn't looking at the view; he was looking at me!

The breath caught in my throat as Ludovico leaned toward me, his energy encompassing me like a cocoon. I felt frozen to the spot. I could barely pull air into my lungs. He leaned closer, then our lips touched. From then on, I was completely love struck.

Ludovico spent every spare minute with me in the remaining days of my trip. He even accompanied me to the obligatory visits to my many older relatives, suffering through endless espressos at quaint kitchen tables while the summer sun continued to blaze outside.

"Wouldn't you rather be at the beach with your friends?" I asked him as we left yet another boring visit.

"What?" he gasped, pulling me in for a big hug, "Don't you get it? I would rather be anywhere that you are."

I hugged him fervently, clinging desperately as I realized that time was slipping away from us. "It's going to be so hard to leave you."

"Let's not think about that now."

But inevitably, my last night arrived. I had thought of every way possible to extend my stay, to no avail. I had to leave. My family and the new school year were waiting for me back in Canada. I had no choice but to leave.

For the first time since I'd arrived in Italy, the rain began to fall over the quiet, quaint town.

"I feel like my heart is breaking," I told Ludovico, tears threatening to spill down my cheeks.

We were sitting in his small hatchback, parked in the piazza, listening to his favorite music CD. The yellow glow of the street lamps cast a sad shadow on the desolate, wet streets.

"I know," he sighed. "I've never felt this way before."

I blinked. Was I hearing him correctly? I hadn't wanted to let myself believe that he could feel as strongly as I did.

"Neither have I," I admitted.

"I . . ." He reached out and took my hand, a pained look in his eyes. "I'm in love with you."

"This is crazy." My tears spilled over. "We hardly know each other, but I'm pretty sure—"

"Yes?" He inched closer.

"—I love you too," I continued through sobs.

Saying goodbye to Ludovico was one of the most painful moments of my life.

"Please, promise me you'll come back soon," he implored. "You must!"

"I will," I was adamant, "at the end of the year."

It was September. How I thought I could make it back to see Ludovico in only three short months, I don't know, but we swore that our love for one another was real and we would be together soon.

I cried for weeks when I got back to Toronto. My parents didn't know what to do with me. They tried to make me see that I couldn't very well pursue a future with a boy that far away, not while I still had my schooling to finish. Besides, they said, I was too young.

I cried until I had no more tears to shed. As the months and then the years passed, it became clear that I would not be returning to Italy anytime soon. Although the pain of missing Ludovico never went away, I pushed it to the back of my heart and continued living my life. I dated other boys, but I never gave my heart away completely.

Ten years later, I realized why.

"Do you remember Ludovico?" my mom asked me casually one morning as I poured a cup of coffee. "He is here visiting, and there will be a party for him at my cousin's place tomorrow night."

My heart skipped a beat. My first love was here? A million conflicting emotions raced through my mind. *Would he even remember me? Had he found someone else to share his passion with?* I didn't think I could endure the embarrassment and disappointment of seeing him with another girl. Though ten years had passed and I'd moved on with my life and forced myself to forget Ludovico, I still had feelings for him. And the thought of seeing him again and not having those feelings reciprocated was more than I could bear.

"Mom, I'm not sure if I can—"

My mother's warning glance stopped me in my tracks. I knew what she was going to say, that it would be rude of me not to go.

"Okay, I'll be there," I acquiesced.

The next night, I said a few polite hellos as I removed my coat, my heart racing with anticipation. I had barely stepped inside when I felt his presence. The hairs stood up on the back of my neck as I glanced across the room at the man I had once declared my eternal devotion to. He stared right back at me, his gaze unreadable. We both broke the connection, hastily looking away. For the next two hours, we avoided each other awkwardly, careful not to glance in the other's direction.

Wanting to retrieve my sweater from the closet, I turned down the corridor into the small front hallway. I was shocked to bang straight into Ludovico.

"Oh, hi." I smiled meekly, nervously tucking my hair behind my ear.

"Hi."

"How are you?" I sounded breathless, even to my own ears, "It's been such a long time."

"I know. It has." His tone was serious. "I've been good. How about you?"

"Good."

The silence was deafening.

"So ten years since you came to Italy?" he asked.

"Yes."

"I remember it like it was yesterday."

I searched his dark eyes, surprised by his words. "I do, too."

Leaning forward, he whispered in my ear, "Nothing's changed for me, Sylvia. I still feel exactly the same."

I closed my eyes, taking in the familiar scent of him. "I do, too."

He pulled me into his arms. "This is ridiculous. I don't want to wait another ten years to see you again."

"I know. But how?"

"I have a few more days here, and then we have to see what we can do about this situation."

His lips lightly grazed against my cheek, and I felt shivers down every nerve in my body. This man was my destiny; I knew it.

"I love you," he whispered.

"And I love you."

I was so excited I could barely make sense of it all. Ludovico was moving to Canada!

It had been a year and a half since we had been reunited—a challenging stretch of long-distance love. Now, he had sent me a ticket to join him in Italy so I help him pack and get organized. We would leave together to begin a new life in my world.

"Can you believe it's finally here?" he embraced me at the airport enthusiastically.

"I can't!" I giggled with excitement. "It's too good to be true."

It was amazing to be together while we scrambled to take care of the many loose ends involved in moving to a different country, but a nagging feeling tugged at my gut. Ludovico would have to say goodbye to everyone— including his ill father—and leave them thousands of miles away . . . for me. Guilt chewed at my insides.

Faces around us were drawn with tension as the final day drew nearer. And then it came: the goodbye.

It was four in the morning on the day of our departure. The night wind whirled eerily in through the open balcony window. Ludovico's mother placed two cups of coffee on the kitchen table and then burst into tears.

"Don't cry, Ma. It's okay," he comforted, embracing the tiny woman as she sobbed.

Then he hugged his father, who whispered, "Don't turn around. Just go."

Tears rolled down my face as I realized what Ludovico was giving up for me, the enormity of his sacrifice and pure love.

It poured rain in Rome that day. Our flight was delayed, and we spent endless hours watching the water pour down the walls in sheets. The sky had never been grayer.

"I'm sorry you have to go through this," I cried.

"No," his voice was laced with sadness. "Don't be. It's just a difficult moment, but this is what I want. I love you."

And just like that, I learned the true meaning of what it meant to love someone. Love isn't only roses, kisses, and poetry. It isn't only sunny days. True love is also sacrifice, compromise, and selflessness. It is storms weathered together.

Six years later, Ludovico and I are happily married with a beautiful baby girl, and we continue to face each storm as it comes our way—hand in hand, heart to heart.

—*Sylvia Suriano-Diodati*

Retiring Bill Pullman

Over the years I've had a low-simmering but perpetual fear of being the Bill Pullman character in my romantic life. For those who don't share this obsession, Bill Pullman is an actor who appeared in a string of 1990s date movies, usually as the guy who doesn't get the girl. Pullman's characters are nice but tend to lack the romantic zing needed to make a woman's heart skip a beat.

In *Singles*, he's the plastic surgeon who tells Bridget Fonda she doesn't need bigger breasts, which empowers her to win back the boyfriend who said she did. In *Sleepless in Seattle*, he's the dull fiancé who Meg Ryan dumps on Valentine's Day so she can pursue a complete stranger. Pullman's date-movie credentials are so entrenched in my psyche that when he showed up as the U.S. president in *Independence Day*, I kept waiting for the First Lady to find someone new. Instead, she died.

Throughout most of our twelve years together, I worried my wife would wake up and realize she'd married her own personal Bill Pullman. As soon as that happened, someone more glamorous would show up to whisk her away. It's a shallow fear and a shallower way to view my wife's affections, but knowing that didn't stop me from feeling it.

Around the same time I first fell in love with my wife, I began to understand I was not her type at all. She preferred sinewy tall men who lived to climb mountain peaks and paddle rapids. I was chubby, short, and hadn't climbed a mountain in my life. But she fell for me because of the strangeness of chemistry and because I made her laugh, was kind to her, and shared my sugary cereal with her between classes. (Never underestimate the power of sugar rushes in a relationship; I think my wife accepted my marriage proposal partly because she had just consumed some really good chocolate.)

Still, even after we became engaged, I worried she would discover my inner Bill Pullman. It was enough to cause panic attacks whenever she suggested we go camping or for a canoe ride. At last, she would see how incompetent I was at such outdoorsy things and fall for whichever rugged guide came out to save us after our canoe tipped!

When it was just the two of us, there was enough time and space for her to talk me down, but now that we have a daughter, my wife has a shorter supply of patience for such idiosyncrasies. Her impatience was enough to make me fear for the worst. The first two years of parenthood are hard on a marriage, and it isn't a great time to indulge in insecurities about a relationship. Sleep deprivation heightens paranoia, and trying to have a conversation with your spouse when your baby is awake is like trying to talk to her from across a crowded subway platform. But now our daughter is old enough to play by herself for a minute or two, and she'll even let us get a word in edgewise, so my wife and I are slowly rediscovering each other.

As parents, if we're lucky, we lose a little of our emotional baggage during our first child's infancy (which is a good thing, because whatever remains hangs like a millstone around our necks). Moping because of an imagined slight or angst over one's career becomes inexpedient when it takes half of a precious nap. There simply isn't enough time, and we decide to drop certain facades of our personality that we no longer find useful.

Taking stock as my daughter's infancy was winding down, I was surprised to discover that I'd left Bill Pullman somewhere along the side of the road. It probably happened gradually each day, as I received a grateful look from my wife whenever I handed her a bowl of soup or a look of relief from her whenever I walked in the door. Once a child comes into the picture, the stakes are raised in a marriage. We no longer look for Mr. or Ms. Right at a time when we are only desperate for Mr. or Ms. Could You Please Hand Me a Diaper and Make Me a Cup of Tea.

An aging actor once said that as we get older, competence increasingly becomes a turn-on. When thinking about marriage, I would replace competence with kindness. For if attraction is the spark that ignites love, it is a thousand daily kindnesses that keep love's flame alive.

Incidentally, I found a recent picture of Bill Pullman on the Internet while writing this essay. He looks older, balder, and fatter. Then again, so does Tom Hanks.

—*Craig Idlebrook*

This story was first published in *Funny Times*, September 2008.

Love and the Un-Romantic

"When were we last romantic?" I ask my husband.

"Huh?"

"You know, when was our last romantic moment?"

He ponders the question, laughs, and then takes a sip of Gatorade from the gallon-sized container in the fridge.

I've been mulling over our twenty-two years of marriage and have yet to come up with a romantic memory. But now I'm determined to because I cannot believe that, in all these years, nothing comes to mind. So I say to myself, *Think, Mary. Think.*

I start with our honeymoon. We had decided to pass on the beaches of St. Thomas and the mountains of the Poconos and instead chose to head for Nashville. We were both gigging musicians, and the sound of "Music City, U.S.A." tickled our ears.

I had bought a red, floral party dress at a vintage thrift shop a few weeks prior to the big day, and I was exuberant and all a-fluff at the airport. We were on our way! But soon I was wincing as I crammed all that lovely red taffeta under my seatbelt on the flight to Tennessee. Fashion maven Betsy Johnson would have been in tears had she seen the wrinkled mess I had become when I walked off the plane. By the time we got to the baggage claim, my feet hurt so much that I scrapped my patent leather shoes for a pair of sneakers before we made our way to a nearby motel.

Tired from the day's excitement and long trip, we decided to stay in for the night and just order a pizza. And, frankly, we were perfectly happy with that.

The rest of our honeymoon was filled with many happy moments, but none that I remember as being truly romantic. Guitar shopping? Our day at the Carl Perkins Railroad Museum? Buying those Elvis mugs we just *had* to have at Graceland? I know for sure that driving over the Memphis–Arkansas Memorial Bridge—just so we could shout, "We're in Arkansas!" out the window of the car—would not be considered textbook romance. Inane. Memorable. Maybe even adorable. But romantic? Not even.

My husband and I are in love, no doubt. Crazy about each other. Two peas in a pod. But truly romantic moments of the traditional variety? None come to mind.

On Valentine's Day we go to our favorite family-run Mexican restaurant and order our no-fail combo plates (number thirteen for him; number seven for me) as our son dips tortilla chips into the salsa and uses his finger to flick the onions back into the dipping bowl.

On each of my birthdays, my husband usually asks, "So what are we doing for your birthday?"—as in "I didn't make any plans." A trip to the bakery for a cake ensues, and I call in the troops for a slice. The cake, as usual, is adorned with "the" candle, a tacky wax mold of the words "Happy Birthday" that has been in my husband's family longer than I have.

I would be remiss if I were to claim that this lack of romantic aptitude is one-sided, all my husband's doing. It is not. I admit that I can't stomach romance novels, that I had a hard time getting through *Pride and Prejudice*, and that I'd cringe if my husband offered me jewelry that bore any semblance to the shape of a heart. (I happily accept, however, any such gifts from my young son.)

Still searching my memory for at least one romantic moment between my husband and me, I think about the time we bought our first—and only—home. Buying your first home would definitely be considered a major romantic event by most young couples. After all, it's a huge (and scary) new step in your coupled life. It's the largest expense you'll ever make together. And it's a major commitment to one another. A home of your own! Where you'll live together and grow old together and maybe even raise kids together. Where you'll have the wild freedom to paint your walls any ghastly color you might want! (I must add, my father told me before he died that the best thing about owning your own home is you can actually say to someone, "Get the he** out of my house!")

When we moved into our humble abode, we had only two pieces of furniture: a pink foam foldout sofa (from my old bedroom at my mother's house) and a five-foot-tall bear statue that I'd found at an antiques store and simply fell in love with.

A couple of days before the house closing, I envisioned what it might be like to spend the first night in our new home: I would light candles and cook a meal in our new kitchen. I would set out a blanket by the fireplace, and we would snack on something delicious using the few dishes we owned. I kept thinking, *Oh, won't it be lovely.*

Unfortunately, my husband, while also excited, happened to be playing baseball with some company employees the day before the house closing and got rammed in the face with an elbow as the runner slid into home plate. So I spent the first night in our new home by myself while my husband recovered from orbital socket surgery in the hospital. In the silence of that empty house, I slept alone on my pink foam coach with that stupid bear looking on mockingly.

The birth of our son might have been a chance for romance. But colic isn't very romantic. I can remember one particular night, walking in my nightgown up and down the block while holding my son who would . . . not . . . stop . . . crying.

My husband pulled up in our car from a long day of work and shouted out to me "What are you doing?"

Through tears, I yelled back with much drama, "It doesn't matter anymore! It doesn't matter anymore!"

He took our crying child from my arms and led me to the car. He put the baby in the baby seat, and drove the three of us to the parkway. (The constant motion of driving will help a colicky baby go to sleep.) Once we hit Exit 25, he turned south toward the beach. Our baby's cries turned into whimpers, and by the time we reached the parking lot of the beach the baby was asleep.

Finally, peace and quiet, with only the sound of the ocean before us. My husband smiled and turned off the car. He took my hand, and we both reclined our seats and fell asleep. Under the stars, in the beach parking lot, we slept—a colicky baby and his two exhausted parents.

Now that I think about it, that's as close to romantic as we've ever been.

These days, I like to think of our boxed lunches on the bleachers of our son's Little League games as our mild attempt at romance.

I guess my husband and I are just anti-romantic, at least in the traditional sense.

Personally, though, I think all that romance stuff is somewhat overrated.

My husband and I are two halves that make a whole. We're happy with each other, our family, our music, our church life, our baseball games (big Mets fans), our bike rides, our son's recitals, and all the various things (exciting and less-than-exciting) that are part of our life together.

We are who we are, and we are in love. He is my guy, and I am his girl. We are perfectly, unashamedly, and unromantically blissful . . . together.

—*Mary C. M. Phillips*

Who Could Ask
for Anything More?

I looked out the window and watched my neighbor remove the last five snowflakes from his driveway. After he used a shovel to scrape the places that the snow blower had missed, he brought out a fine-bristled broom to scrape up any snowflakes still caught in the rough pavement.

Just then my husband came in the back door, covered with more snow than he had removed and announcing that if I really wanted to get out of the driveway I should take the truck, which had four-wheel drive.

"Gee, did you notice our neighbor's driveway?" I asked, trying not to sound like I was comparing the two.

"Hello? Can you believe that guy?" my husband chuckled. "Isn't it enough that you can eat off his driveway in the summer? Does he know he's making the rest of us look bad?"

"He's probably just fussy when it comes to his driveway," I said, even though I knew better. In the summer, his lawn not only is raked, it's also combed, and the trees are manicured to the point where he removes any leaves that don't look quite right and dresses the chipmunks in formal attire. They're really quite adorable. He scrapes the lichen off the tree trunks, and his birds are not only well fed but always look neat as a pin to boot.

"I can't imagine what the inside of his house looks like," my husband yelled from the living room through a mouthful of potato chips. "I bet he drives his wife crazy."

Oh, I bet he doesn't, I thought, as I cleaned up the pathway of chips my husband had dropped, à la Hansel and Gretel, from the kitchen to his easy chair. *I bet he wipes his feet at the door and then shakes the rug out, washes and puts away the bowl he used for a midnight snack, and makes the bed in the morning as soon as his wife gets up to go to the bathroom*, I thought, allowing myself to dream. *That might bother some people, but it sounds like a little bit of heaven to me.*

I rescued the half-eaten bag of chips from my husband's lap when he jumped up to cheer for his favorite team, brushing a handful of crumbs off his shirt and onto the carpet.

"You know, ants like potato chips," I said, trying not to sound like a nag.

"In the winter?" he replied without taking his eyes off the game. "That's what I'm talking about!" he yelled as the Patriots scored a touchdown.

I returned the bag of chips to its rightful spot in the pantry, and contemplated getting out the vacuum and running it across the living room and up the front of my husband's sweatshirt. I'm sure he figures that as long as everything gets vacuumed by spring, our house will be safe from unwanted wildlife.

When the game was over, my husband came into the kitchen.

"Hey, I think I'll check out the movie channel," he said. "Or would you like to watch one of our own? How about *Casablanca*? We haven't seen that one in a long time."

He got halfway down the hallway, stopped, and turned around, "Any idea where it is?"

"Yes, it's in the video bookshelf, top row, third one from the left, right next to *Caddy Shack*," I answered without hesitation.

"Wow, you have our movies in alphabetical order? When did you do that?"

He grabbed the movie and got ready to settle down for the night. "Are you ready?" he said as he reached for the light switch.

I grabbed the rest of the potato chips and a bowl that had been on the counter since the night before. I picked up a couple pillows off the floor and moved some of the golf magazines from the top of the coffee table to create a space for my feet.

"Here, let's cover up those tootsies of yours before they get cold," he said as he threw the blanket over my bare feet. "It wouldn't do for my little Ingrid Bergman to catch cold."

I snuggled up against my husband, chips and all.

He isn't perfect, I thought to myself, *but seriously, who is?*

As he put his arm around me, he gave me a little squeeze and whispered, "Here's looking at you, kid," holding out the bowl for me to reach and help myself to a few chips.

He gave me a wink, and I melted into his side. In an imperfect world, I had the most perfect guy, crumbs and all. Who could ask for anything more?

—*Beverly Lessard*

Live, Love, Laugh

My twenty-two-year-old husband slipped off his sweats, wiggled into yet another hospital gown, and shuffled toward his bed. The growth of the tumor below his left shoulder blade bowed his back, putting more pressure on one foot, giving his walk a beat—sort of a shuffle, thump, shuffle, thump sound.

"Move your hambone, Ron," I said, trying to tie the gown in the back.

"What one part of me would be ham?" he asked with a grin that had refused to be chased away by the pain.

"You're right; you're one big ham," I agreed.

When we had arrived early that morning to the doctor's office for his chemotherapy treatment, the nurse said his white blood cell count had dropped. Again. The doctor ordered us to go to the hospital, and we settled into our usual routine for such days.

We found M*A*S*H listed on the TV's onscreen guide and prepared to count how many episodes we could find in a row.

My husband pushed the button to raise the head of the bed, scooted over, and patted the turned-down sheet, requesting a snuggle. I kicked off my shoes and hesitated. We weren't in the usual hospital on our regular floor, and I didn't know these nurses. This time they had put him in the cancer ward. As soon as I gave into the request and sat on the bed with him, the door opened and his nurse appeared.

"Ron, I'll be your nurse today," the young woman said.

"Good. Too bad a nurse-a-day doesn't keep the doctor away," Ron answered.

She half-smiled and opened the chart.

"Who is your doctor?" she asked, mostly to herself, while flipping through the chart.

"Aww, you know him," Ron said bobbing his hairless brow up and down like Charlie Chaplin on chemo. "He's the one wearing white, with twelve interns following him, trying to heal the sick."

"His name is . . . ?" she began, not quite understanding who she was dealing with.

"Don't worry. You won't see him much in here. I seem to present some kind of challenge. I make his complex more complex," Ron said.

The nurse peered over the chart and closed it. *Smart lady*, I thought. She realized reading with Ron in the room was like trying to enjoy a novel and jumping from an airplane at the same time.

"How are you feeling?" the poor woman tried a different tactic in an attempt to do her duty.

My husband grabbed my thigh. "With my hands. Isn't that right, honey?" he asked me with a wide grin sporting dried, chapped lips—an effect of the chemo, "I feel with my hands."

I could smell his metallic breath, the way it had smelled since he started the treatments.

I said nothing. I knew my role: Mindy to his Mork. On cue, I rolled my eyes and looked the other direction.

She put the chart under her arm and said, "Oooookaaaay then. I'll return with your tray."

"Well, Ron, we'll be left alone today," I said. "I think you frightened her. She looks new."

"Fine with me. A day alone with you anywhere is paradise."

He can't be serious, I thought. I looked at him evenly, but all the Charlie Chaplin mimicry had disappeared.

A few minutes later, the nurse returned with a tray. Instead of ignoring me like most of the nurses had in the past, she looked me up and down as if

I were a pear tree growing apples. I thought it was because I was still snuggled beside my hubby on the bed. When she left without any conversation, I felt relieved.

Just two minutes later, the door opened again and the nurse brought in a second tray. "I know you weren't planning a hospital visit today, so I thought you might be hungry, too," the nurse said with a smile.

"Uh, thanks . . . Thanks," I stammered.

I knew rules prohibited visitors from eating even the leftover food on the patients' trays, and never before had a nurse brought an extra tray for me. I searched for a reason for her actions. I thought about my clothes and my appearance. I wore nice gym shoes, a name brand. My jeans weren't faded or holey or anything other than, well, jeans. I wore the sweater my mother-in-law had given me for my birthday; it was new. I had put a bit of makeup on before coming, and my hair had been cut at a salon. I didn't look needy. I couldn't understand why she had brought me the food tray.

I shook off the list of her ulterior motives forming in my head. Having breakfast with my husband, watching M*A*S*H, and not watching Ron puke all afternoon felt like a reprieve from the agenda we had expected. Although we knew he needed the chemo, we almost celebrated during breakfast. After all, he had lost about 60 pounds, so it was good for him to eat and keep it down for a change.

Together, we weighed 260 pounds. We thought of most things that way—together.

While we ate, the nurse returned again. She brought in supplies.

"You did bring a comb?" Rob asked, rubbing his bald head.

This time she smiled a full smile with one eyebrow raised as if to say, "Okay, I got your number now."

Before the M*A*S*H episode ended, she returned to chat, making it hard to watch the conclusion. Not that we cared, really. TV was just a distraction, and a real human to talk with in a hospital room was a better distraction.

After she left, I asked Ron, "Doesn't she have other patients? You've never been given so much attention."

"Maybe you'd better ask for a recliner and stay the night. I think she has a crush on me."

I laughed. "Yeah," I replied slowly. "Must be the lack of hair. It's a real turn-on."

"Makes me look tough," he said as he tried to flex an AWOL muscle.

The nurse returned. Ron and I suppressed smiles.

She stood at the end of the bed and looked at Ron with much consideration. "I wouldn't ask this if I didn't like you," she began.

Ron nudged me with his elbow.

The nurse continued. "I need you to do a favor for me, Ron. I need your bedside manner. The young man next door is just a couple of years older than you. He has cancer of the nose and throat. They removed his nose two days ago, and he hasn't turned on the light, spoken to anyone, or eaten anything since. I need you to go and cheer him up."

Ron wiped his mouth with his napkin and said, "Oooookaaaay," with a twinkle in his eye. He stood up and shuffled away.

The nurse said to me, "I'd appreciate it if you didn't talk to the young man next door and if you stay out of sight, at least at first."

The woman who had brought me a tray now didn't like me for some reason? The extra attention, the request to go help another patient, and now her wanting me out of the way just wasn't adding up to "normal" nurse behavior.

"You see," she continued, "his wife walked in his room the day before his surgery, their two-year-old in her arms, and laid her wedding ring on the side table. She told him she would be in California with her relatives. Before she left, she gave me her phone number and asked me to call when he died. She said she'd come back to make the funeral arrangements."

Then the nurse looked at me with those x-ray eyes again. I returned her stare. She was about my age and wore no wedding ring.

"Why are you different than the other wife, I wonder?" she asked quietly, as if talking to herself.

I felt like a timepiece on a watchmaker's workbench having my gears inspected. The nurse wanted to know what made me tick. None of us really know the answer to that one.

Past the curtain I saw Ron walk up to the door. I stepped behind the curtain as best I could so the guy without a nose wouldn't see me.

"We're going to the weight room," Ron called in. "My new friend likes to lift weights."

"Heard you," the nurse said, flashing an approving smile at Ron.

"You're wondering what makes a marriage work even in the tough times?" I asked.

"Yes."

She turned to look at me again. She saw me as someone possessing guru-on-top-of-the-mountain wisdom, and she had no right to expect so much of me. I was just a regular person in an irregular situation.

I answered with a chuckle. "I don't have that kind of wisdom to teach about love or devotion or some universal truth. I'm not Kahlil Gibran. Not even close. I'm not even Helen Steiner Rice."

"Okay, maybe you have one answer. What makes you two stay together?"

"Me? I just want to see what he'll do next."

She smirked and nodded. As she left the room, she probably thought we were just a pair of smart-mouthed people who couldn't live without each other. But I knew I had to learn to live without him. Meanwhile, I functioned as his juicer, helping him squeeze life out of every moment.

Ron returned, ready to rest. He looked paler than he had a couple of hours before.

I flipped through the channels to another episode of M*A*S*H. On a piece of paper I had placed on his tray, I wrote down the time and "episode #2."

"How much did you lift in the weight room?" I asked.

"Five pounds. The guys at the firehouse would have laughed," he said. "But it doesn't matter what two people do together, all that matters is the two people find something to do together. Now let me hold you," he said, patting the bed.

The theme song for M*A*S*H had started to play.

—*Tami Absi*

Love Imitates Art

Above our heads the painterly clouds dab the sky, perfect as an Impressionist landscape. I consult the visitor map and point the way, my sandals padding the grass beside my husband's black sneakers, but my step is springier than his. With a glance, I take in an image of Bart. His downcast eyes and solemn beard seem to lengthen his Russian-icon face. Well, I think, at least I got him out of the house.

Barely an hour before, my husband lay camped out on the family room sofa. He didn't feel like golfing, he said. He didn't feel like going to the gym. He didn't feel like doing anything.

"It's a beautiful day," I offered, gesturing toward the window where the September sun washed in.

"I don't know," he sighed. "Faith, I just feel so . . . so betrayed."

"Me too. You used to say Susan was the sister you never had. Remember how you brought her soup when she was sick? And for months, she was planning this."

My husband is the only insurance agent I know who plays Hindu chant CDs in his office. "It's so soothing," he says. But nothing could calm him this tumultuous week. Five days earlier, he'd made a shocking discovery about a saleswoman we both trusted, not just as a coworker but also as a friend. Now, Bart had filed a lawsuit against a person he used to have lunch with every week. Friends called to say, "Bart's too nice of a guy."

I thought I knew what we needed: a change of scenery, something beautiful to wipe away the ugliness of the past week and replace it with color and texture. I thought first of the art museum. Although art is more my interest than his, I love the way my husband's eyes crinkle as he savors my enthusiasm over a work by Cezanne, Monet, Kandinsky, or Noguchi. But it was such a beautiful day. A park maybe or an arboretum?

Then I remembered a place we'd been meaning to see, a sculpture park several friends had raved about, about 45 minutes from home.

"How about Grounds for Sculpture?"

He shifted his body, adjusted a throw pillow.

"It'll do you good to get some fresh air and sunshine." Even I recoiled at the chirp in my voice, sharp and artificial.

Miraculously, he rolled into a sitting position, sighed, and reached for his sneakers. He was only humoring me, but I hoped that art and nature would work their magic in spite of his reluctance.

An hour later, we follow the winding path through the trees, past a chrome behemoth that resembles a double-helix strand of DNA. I squat down to fit the entire sculpture into the frame of my digital camera, wobbling a bit as I get up.

At parties, when people ask, "So how did you two meet?" Bart and I grin and answer almost in unison, "At a Puerto Rican pig roast." Our story is always a hit.

Some thirty years ago, I was a shy graduate student in jeans and a peasant blouse, just off a bad relationship. A friend invited me to a party at the home of a couple I barely knew. She thought it would do me good to get "back out there." Having nothing better to do on a Saturday night, I made my entrance to a living room full of strangers. Seeing no available seat, I plunked myself down to sit cross-legged on the floor, wedged between the artsy freeform coffee table and someone else's shoes.

As the mass of voices around me sifted into individual conversations, it dawned on me that everyone else was speaking Spanish. So I sat there on the floor, longing for subtitles and smiling a smile that felt carved into my cheeks.

Then I saw him: a bearded guy with sleepy eyes right out of a portrait by Modigliani, slouching against the wall, wearing a look as lost as mine.

The sweet scent of roasting pork and a shout of excitement accompanied the hostess's friends and cousins as they hauled in a huge plank bearing something I'd only seen in cartoons: an entire freshly roasted pig, complete with apple in mouth. As the paper plates were passed around, amid rapid-fire Spanish dialogue, the first stumbling words passed between me and the man I would marry.

Back then, I wrote poetry and dabbled with a paintbrush. He was a philosophy major, stunned to find himself stepping into the family insurance business after his father's heart attack. He played basketball and read Sartre "for fun."

Eventually I gave him a key to my first apartment. Once we had a fight. Every night for over a week I checked my answering machine in vain for one of his goofy phone messages. Then one night I trudged home from work and noticed the light glowing under my door. A note greeted me in his scratchy handwriting: "Don't be scared. It's only me, the Doctor J of the Insurance World." Just like that, my mood melted, my body lightened, I flung the door open and raced to him.

In the lush gardens of Grounds for Sculpture, we linger beside a beautifully landscaped pond. A ghostly bronze face hovers over the face of the water, brooding in the soft mist.

"She looks like the Lady of the Lake," I say, a reference to a character in English literature, which, I realize after I say it, he might be too distracted to pick up on.

Amidst the green, a flash of rose catches my eye. I stray from the path to investigate. "Wait, Bart," I say to his back.

Lost in thought, he plunges on ahead of me.

"Bart," I repeat, a little louder.

He doesn't even hear me. I know in his mind he's second-guessing his actions, worrying that the business his father and he built might be in jeopardy.

"*Bart!*" I scamper up to him and touch his shoulder. "Check this out!"

Taking his hand, I lead him into the trees. Our eyes adjust to the mixture of shade and light. We seem to have interrupted a conversation. Two men in nineteenth-century morning coats laze on the grass, the one on the right wearing a straw hat and gesturing with one expansive arm. The woman seated with them looks straight at me. Her fingers rest on her chin. Her skin glows in the dapples of sun. She's naked.

Instantly, we smile. We're standing inside a painting translated into three dimensions, the famous and enigmatic "Luncheon on the Grass," by Édouard Manet. The real-life trees, river, sunlight, and boat in the background all perfectly re-enact the painting I know so well. Crumpled behind the nude lady are her hat and flouncy blue dress. Apples and bread spill toward us from inside a wicker basket.

I hand Bart my camera. "Take my picture as if I'm in the painting!"

I jump into the scene between the naked woman and her luncheon companions.

Bart is fumbling with the camera. He has only come here to humor me, I realize. Yet I see those eyes crinkle; he seems to enjoy my enjoyment, so maybe it's doing him some good anyhow.

I jump out of the picture, instruct him, then hop back in.

Snap.

We were married the day after my twenty-fifth birthday, in an informal ceremony in my parents' living room. My dress cost thirty-five dollars, and when people commented that I still used my maiden name, Bart quipped, "I didn't change my name either."

On our twenty-fifth anniversary, the day after my fiftieth birthday, I woke up in a hotel in the Bahamas, our three brown-eyed sons asleep in the next room dreaming of a snorkeling day.

Rolling over, I said, with a hiccup of laughter, "I just realized something: I've been married exactly half my life."

"You've been a good sport about it," my husband said, with a kiss.

In the park, a family of live peacocks scampers out of our way. We pass a rough-hewn Stonehenge object decorated with carved whirls and swirls, and a fiberglass Loch Ness monster flailing its tentacles out of a fountain. I'm lost in exploration, the music of water playing over soft rapids. Then I make out a form in the shadow, my husband on a marble bench, his dark eyes turned inward. Suddenly, I'm aware of the sun's heat pressing on the top of my head.

What am I trying to do, I ask myself. *I can't force him to lift his eyes, to look, to smile. I can't make him get over his frustration by artificial means. Maybe it isn't right to distract him from his loss. He has a right to his feelings.*

"I used to think I was a good judge of character," he says as I approach him.

"Come on," I say, prying him off the bench. "Just a little farther."

And then I add, "You sensed something was wrong, remember? You kept saying, 'I'm concerned about Susan. She always makes excuses not to have lunch with me anymore.' Now we know why. She couldn't face you. Her conscience was bothering her."

We talk as we walk, that familiar glow between us. I don't have anything profound to say or any solutions to offer, but maybe, like the Hindu chant music playing in his office, after half a lifetime of practice my presence just calms him down. If there is a secret to our longevity, maybe it is in this.

"We'll be all right," I tell him.

At the top of the observation tower, I snap a photo of Bart, a slightly more relaxed look on his face, as in the background the sun and clouds knit together.

Our feet back on the ground, my husband says my name. "Faith?"

"Yeah?"

"Thanks for marrying me."

Suddenly, in front of us, a grassy hill arises, dotted with bright red poppies. A woman stands on top of the hill, captured in the instant when she whirls around to glance at us, her long skirts swirling in the wind, her lips parted, scarf flying, green parasol tipped.

A shared breath escapes both of our mouths. "Wow."

We both recognize this as a 3-D replica of Claude Monet's painting "The Stroll." The steep slope evokes the upward perspective of the vertical canvas. The woman at the top of the hill is Monet's wife, Camille. Throughout their years together, Monet painted Camille more often than any other model, his brush snatching single moments before they evaporated into the air, right up until his last depiction of her, a work called, "Camille Monet on Her Deathbed." Yet, here she is, high above us, alive, fresh, and young.

My sandals keeping pace with his sneakers, in this place that marries art and nature, I soak in a little of what the Impressionists knew. That a shared moment is a complete composition. That if we stroll together today, as colors flicker in our eyes, then yesterday and tomorrow will take care of themselves.

As we pass, Madame Monet seems to smile at us, just as her husband painted her, with her young son Jean partly visible in the background, dancing between the sun and wind on a hill sparkling with poppies.

—*Faith Paulsen*

The artworks described in this piece include "Dejeuner Déjà Vu" and "Poppied Hill," by Seward Johnson, at Grounds for Sculpture in Harrison, New Jersey.

Willow Weep No More

They have seventy-one years of marriage between the two of them, although together they just celebrated eighteen.

Mom says, "He is my third marriage but my first husband."

My parents, Trudi and Marty, met in 1963, when both were involved in the Midwest region of United Synagogue Youth. Mom lived in St. Louis and Dad lived in Des Moines. Over the next two years they saw each other only six times, but they sent letters daily. When Mom arrived at camp the summer of 1965, she saw Marty holding hands with another girl. She cried for two weeks.

In the fall, she started her senior year of high school. In art class she expressed her feelings through painting with a self-portrait entitled "Willow Weep for Me."

The next summer, Mom and Marty saw each other at camp again. Although they did trade a glance or two, they did not exchange a single word.

Two more years passed, and no letters passed between them. Eventually, Mom accepted an engagement ring from another. Then, on a Thursday night, she received a phone call.

"Don't get married," Marty said. "Come to Des Moines and meet my parents."

She agreed and went to tell her parents.

Her mother's reaction was quite simple. "We have two-hundred-fifty Cornish hens ordered for your wedding in two days."

The trip to Des Moines never happened.

After fourteen years of marriage and three daughters (I am the middle one) my mom's marriage ended. After some time and consideration, she decided to find Marty. Going about things the old-fashioned way, without the luxury of Google, she talked with friends and went to the library for phone books. She took a chance and called the now "Dr. Rosenfeld" at his office. It was a simple conversation.

"Hi. I'm divorced, and I heard you were, too."

His reaction was not what she had hoped for.

"I remarried, and we just had a baby," Marty said.

Again, she hung the self-portrait on the wall . . . and wept.

My younger sister, Tiffany, followed in my mother's footsteps and joined the same region of USY that Mom had been in almost thirty years earlier. She attended the fall conference in Des Moines. One evening during a large group dinner, a gentleman in a light-blue sport jacket walked on stage and, amid the hundreds of teenagers, took the microphone and simply asked, "Does anyone out there know Trudi Lasky?"

My sister, very shy and quite surprised, raised her hand, stood up, and said hesitantly, "That is my mom."

Marty introduced himself to Tiffany and explained how he knew Mom (although I am pretty certain he left out many details). She snapped a few pictures and accepted his phone number, assuring him that she would pass it along to Mom when the weekend conference was over.

But my sister was a little uncertain. Mom was in the middle of her second divorce, and that marriage, like her first, was far from healthy. Tiffany wondered whether she should develop the pictures and give Mom the phone number now or wait until some semblance of normal returned to our lives. Then again, what was normal? Why not give this a shot and move ahead with a new normal?

Tiffany told Mom about her surprise visitor in Des Moines, and the two decided they should develop the film immediately. After all, Mom had not seen Marty in almost three decades. However, by that time, the new puppy had decided the roll of film was a chew toy, so there were no pictures. But on Tiffany's urging, Mom called the number, and although she had no picture, she finally heard Marty's voice again.

During their second phone conversation, he proposed and she accepted. The ring arrived in the mail later that week.

Months went by, and just like teenagers, Mom and Marty talked on the phone every night for hours. We all started to notice that this "new normal" could, and did, involve smiles and happiness. The willow tree was no longer weeping. The only problem: he was in Des Moines and she was in St. Louis.

Fall arrived, and it was time for Mom to take me to college at the University of Iowa—coincidentally, only two hours east of Des Moines. After checking into the hotel, Mom and I had just sat down to relax when the front desk called to say there was something wrong with the credit card Mom had used to make the reservation. She let the desk clerk know she was on her way down to straighten things out.

When the elevator doors opened to the lobby, there stood Marty with two dozen red roses. He quickly explained that there was nothing wrong with her credit card; it had all been a ploy to get her to the lobby. I will never forget the image of my mom, happier than I had ever seen her, in the arms of her true love. It was kismet; meant to be.

Many years have passed since my Mom and Dad finally got married. (Although not my biological father, Marty has been "Dad" to me in every sense of the word.) Like all marriages, they have gone through some rough spots, but nothing could have prepared them for what was to come.

In December 2009, Dad was involved in an incident that left him a quadriplegic. He was on a ventilator in an intensive care unit for six weeks. Mom rarely left his side. She became his advocate, his voice, his calming presence, his angel. They have since left the hospital and for the last three months (and counting) have been at a remarkable rehabilitation facility.

When Mom feels angry, hopeless, exhausted, helpless, frustrated, or any negative emotion, I simply ask her, "Do you still love him?"

She answers me without hesitating. "I did not think I could love him more than I have my entire life, but I do."

In Hebrew, the letters of the alphabet also have a numerical value. The Hebrew word for life, *chai*, has the numerical value of eighteen. In February, at the remarkable rehabilitation facility, my parents celebrated their eighteenth anniversary. For them, life has started again.

Although my mother's self-portrait is now hanging in my living room, I know the willow is not weeping. It is a constant reminder to me that the power of love can go beyond the past as well as the present to create a beautiful future—such as this "new normal" that has returned my mom to the arms of her true love, her first true husband.

—*Suzanne Yoder*

Love Shack

I'm quiet. That's what people who don't know me say, anyway. I spend hours plotting my next verbal expression. I write conversation starters in my journal. I record funny things I should have said in a situation in which all I could think to do at the time was smile and nod. When I'm in a group of people, I observe, I contemplate.

Joe likes to talk. He's the life of the party, the guy with the jokes, the guy who says what everyone else is thinking but is too afraid to say. He has no inner monologue. Before he has a chance to think about what he's going to say, it just blurts right out of his mouth. "Diarrhea of the mouth," I call it.

I'm sweet. Even people who know me say that.

He's whatever it is that's the opposite of sweet. Well, except with me, but no one is supposed to know that. Don't tell anyone I let his secret out.

The day we met was an unusual one for me. I was talkative. It was a typical day for him; he was interruptive. I walked into Radio Shack to buy a prepaid phone card for a weekend out of town with my friends. I told Scott, my friend behind the counter, all about the concert we were planning to see. I told him how excited I was. Then I told him that one of the friends I was headed out of town with just happened to have broken my heart the day before. I had found out that he wasn't interested in me in "that way" and that he had gone out with both of my girlfriends from work on different nights the same weekend he'd taken me out.

I told Scott that I hated men—except him, of course. He didn't count because he was my friend. I told him I was done with the stupid pursuit of Mr. Right. I told him about my plan to be the crazy lady with fifty-seven cats and a porch swing where I could sit and yell at whippersnappers who strayed onto my lawn.

Scott shook his head and laughed. "You've already got the crazy part," he said.

"I'm not crazy," I told him. "Men are crazy. And stupid. They pretend they like you when they really don't just so they can take your heart and break it into fifty million tiny pieces. Then they apologize, and you melt. Your heart gets glued back together for half a minute—just long enough for them to break it apart again."

The new guy at The Shack—the one with the intentional baldness, the surfer dude necklace, the strong cologne, and the runny mouth—interrupted my hateful spiel. "That's because you're dating boys," he said.

I shot him a glare and continued my tirade. "And then the ones who aren't out to break your heart act like they just can't live if you aren't by their side 24/7. They act like—"

"Okay, here's what you want in a man," the new guy interrupted. "You want a guy who is nice but not too nice. If you wanted one of those sweet and sensitive ones, you'd want to date girls. Right?"

He didn't wait for my response before he continued. "You want a guy who will open doors for you but will also let you do things for yourself . . . "

I glared at him as he proceeded to tell me everything I had ever wanted in a man.

"And you're glaring at me like that because I'm right and you know I'm right, but you don't want to let on that I'm right. Right?"

"No!" I protested.

He smiled victoriously and slid a piece of paper across the counter. "Here. Write down your name and I'll freak you out even more."

I looked at him questioningly and then wrote my first name only on the paper.

He picked it up and studied my penmanship as he ran his hand over his goatee and hummed. "Hmm . . ."

"Your letters curve to the left. This tells me that you are somewhat introverted. The loops in your letters tell me that you are happy and bubbly . . ."

He was right on. And yes, it did freak me out. I told him so, too. Before I walked out the door I looked over my shoulder and said, "You're weird. Stay away from me."

But I couldn't stay away from him.

The next week I was back in the store for another phone card. I did need one, but what I really wanted was to see that new guy. This time I examined his empty left ring finger and noted the name printed on the pin on his shirt.

"How was the concert?" Joe asked.

"Awesome," I said as I tried to keep my cool.

"How were things with that guy all weekend?"

I laughed. "Fun for us. Miserable for him. We didn't talk to him, and he kept asking if we were mad at him."

"That's pretty cold," he said.

"Maybe. But so was what he did to us."

"You know, you need a guy who—"

"I know," I interrupted. "You told me what I needed last week, remember?"

The speaker was speechless. I grabbed my phone card and left.

Every time I went into the store, we talked a little bit more. One day he ripped off a piece of receipt paper and jotted down his number. "Here," he said as he slid it across the counter. "You can call me sometime if you want. If you ever need to talk to someone about how stupid men are. Or whatever."

I kept his number in my wallet for weeks. Throughout those weeks, I studied The List. You know what I'm talking about: The List of What I Want in a Man. Every woman has one. And if they don't—well, they should.

There were a few things on The List that didn't quite fit him. I drew a small X for "nope" next to "must have a cat," "must be in a rock band," and "must have blue eyes." However, a lot of the things on the list fit him perfectly. I made giant check marks next to the good qualities he possessed: charm, sense of humor, smarts, a job . . .

But there was one item on the list I didn't know about, so I finally called him. After the preliminary "How ya doin's," I asked the question: "What's your last name?"

"Hozey," he said.

I threw up in my mouth. "Hozey? Seriously?"

"Yep," he said. "Why?"

I looked at The List in my lap and drew a great big red X next to "must not have a stupid last name."

"Oh. No reason," I said.

I don't know what it was. Maybe it was the confidence and charisma. Maybe it was the cologne and surfer dude necklace. Maybe it was the way he made me want to punch him every time he opened his mouth. Or maybe it was the fact that he always seemed to know what I was thinking and blurted it out before I even had a chance to spend an hour contemplating how I was going to say it. I don't know what exactly it was, but a little over a year later I walked into the Social Security office and officially changed my last name to something stupid.

—*Michelle Hozey*

A Room of His Own

My husband's room is at the back of our apartment, next to the kitchen. How many times have I walked by and wanted to haul out his clutter and hurl it into the trash? Sometimes, I've kicked a box out of my way en route to his desk or thrown a stack of papers on the bed because I couldn't find the latest PTA notice. But I controlled the impulse to clean up. If he wanted to spend the better part of his days in clutter, so be it.

Back in Harry's bachelor place, it took many arguments to convince him that a coat rack did not belong in front of a bay window. Now, cardboard boxes are stacked higher than the windowsill. The guest bed and Harry's desk occupy most of the nine square feet; what's left is a three-foot-wide corridor where he swivels around on his office chair. He spends hours in front of the computer, his back to the door, slumped from bad posture. When he talks to friends on the phone, he rests his calves on the desk. Then his laughter rings over into the kitchen. For more serious conversations, he slams his door shut, especially when our toddler decides that Daddy's threshold is the best place to toot his fire engine.

The walls are unadorned; there's not even a bulletin board. Whatever artwork the kids bestow on Daddy is scattered on the desk, curling from the humidity that seeps in from the kitchen or yellowing from sunlight. The kids' paper frogs with glued-on buttons share desk space with unopened charity solicitations, the Paul Fredrick shirt catalog, pink car-repair receipts, doctors' business cards, and Post-it notes from me. A Plexiglas bin overflows with coins. Cardboard cartons, a shredder, and filing boxes crowd the space under the desk.

Once in a while, Harry surveys the scene, leans back in his chair, hands crossed behind his head, looks at me, and moans: "What am I supposed to do with this mess?"

"Clean it up," I'll say, leaning in the doorway, hand on hip.

"Yes, but how?"

"You take a pile, go through it piece by piece, throw out what you don't need, and file the rest."

"Yes, but I can't do that without you. I need you to help me."

So far we have left it at that, both of us unwilling to commit what little time we have as a twosome to cleaning up his room. We'd rather hang out and talk.

I tease him that, here in our Chicago apartment, he has recreated the disarray of his father's wholesale shop, where out-of-fashion sweaters, skirts, and scarves were never weeded out but wandered up another level on the shelves that reached to the fifteen-foot-high ceiling.

Harry grew up in the back room of that store in Munich, Germany. A cardboard box was his playpen. The room smelled of dust that had absorbed years of cigarette smoke, textile dye, and polyurethane bag odor. Of the secretaire desk, only the hutch door with its stained glass tulip window was visible under heaps of order forms, customs declarations, and shipping documents. Oil-heater grime had blackened the walls.

Maybe that is why Harry insisted the walls in our condo be painted white and he is reluctant to hang anything on the walls. His room now does not have a particular smell, but when I snuggle into one of the sweatshirts cast off on the bed, I breathe in traces of his Paco Rabanne Eau de Toilette. Sometimes we push the *PC World*, *Popular Mechanics*, *Car & Driver*, and *Men's Health* magazines on the bed against the wall, lie down, and watch a DVD movie on his computer.

One night I rested there, icing a bruised shin.

"Would you like a cookie with your coffee?" Harry asked from the kitchen.

While I waited for him, my gaze drifted over the flickering screen, the desk lamp that bends down too low, the picture of his father half hidden behind a cup stuffed with ballpoint pens, the box that covers part of the window. And I felt transported to a time when we were still girlfriend and boyfriend, when I woke up early and lay next to him, contemplating his bedroom: the naked floor-to-ceiling windows, the sleeves of his suit jackets queued up on the coat rack, the bare walls, the king-size mattress on the floor.

It dawned on me then that, in the little room next to the kitchen, Harry had preserved his "this-is-how-I-live" identity, not hindered by my decorating efforts or the family that has grown up around him. I recoiled at how often I had been tempted to reach in, pluck paper after paper, and drop it in a plastic bag. I was grateful I had never torn this room apart in a frenzy of homemaking, had not destroyed the habitat of the twenty-five-year-old I fell in love with. He still lives among all those boxes. It is his room.

—*Annette Gendler*

Wildly in Love

With my husband by my side, safety is never an issue. Michael could get us out of a tight situation with such ease and finesse that we'd be out of danger long before I'd realized any peril had existed. The day Michael looks alarmed, we are guaranteed goners. Michael exemplifies "the three Rs": rugged, resourceful, and risk taker—qualities I find endearing in people other than myself.

Marrying a scuba diver, mountain climber, and cross-country hiker granted me a thrill by association. For eight years, I've encouraged his free-spirited activity, flashing him the thumbs up from the safety of the shoreline, the window of a luxury cabin, or the well-traveled pathway at the foot of the mountain. While he dives into the throes of adventure, I dive under a throw made of chenille to read a great book until Michael returns to share his close encounter with the protective mother bear and her cubs; the treacherous mountain trail with a drop-off, where his foot wandered a bit from the path; or the copperhead that slithered under his boot. I acknowledge a twinge of jealousy when listening to what I could've seen firsthand.

"Did you enjoy your leisurely bath?" he asks, with too much emphasis on the word "leisurely."

"Well, yeah, I guess it was okay," I say.

"Good. I'm glad you could relax while I was scaling the cliff."

The need to correct his false perceptions of my complete safety within the cabin's walls overtakes me, and I point to my calf. "See that?"

"What?"

"That cut. Used a new razor in the tub. Bled all over the place." I throw him a sideways glance. "Thought I'd need a Band-Aid."

"Hmm, that so?" he says while making a high-protein drink to reload for his next death-defying feat.

"Yeah. And my pumice stone . . . I swear it has teeth."

He ignores me while he checks his hiking gear.

Annoyed, I thrust my hand near his face. "Have you ever tried to give yourself a manicure without the proper tools?"

He fails to respond to my plight, obviously not recognizing my challenges when holed up in the mountains. Then, suddenly, I'm bored with myself.

"Would you like to join me on a hike tomorrow?" he asks. "Maybe we'll see a black bear."

The excursion sounds outlandishly dangerous. It's not that I don't like nature; I do—from a distance. I could sit and look at wildlife for hours as long as a screened porch, an Adirondack chair, and a café latte are involved. I'm not one to find excitement as the lone person in the forest, noting changes in the wind currents, identifying different types of animal scat, or acknowledging various species of plant life while I'm carrying nothing more than a canteen of water and a granola bar in the event that unforeseen circumstances force me to spend the night in the woods. Instead, I stay indoors and indulge in niceties for myself while Michael partakes in his dangerous, testosterone-packed jaunts. After all, if I'm going to be a young widow, I need to stay somewhat attractive.

Yet, when I look at my husband's peaceful demeanor, I feel the urge to mingle with the fragrant rhododendron, stumble upon a refreshing waterfall, and gaze admiringly at a wide-eyed doe with her wobbly legged fawn at her side.

Michael says, "Today, a man spotted a bobcat."

With those words, a snarling cat perched atop a rock and ready to strike an unsuspecting hiker replaces my image of the precious fawn. "Bobcat? Aren't those dangerous?"

"Can be." He looks at me. "If you're worried, maybe you should stay here."

And I do. All week. As we leave the luxury cabin to return home from the mountains, I vow that next time will be different, promising to let myself go forth into the wild.

I should not have made that vow aloud.

Upon our return to Missouri, my husband suggests that we ease into my promise with a simple canoe trip down the Meramec River. I agree to go, even though rain is forecast. After all, I don't want to look like my same old, unadventurous self.

The ninety-minute drive allows time for contemplation. "What if we capsize?" I ask.

"Then we get wet," he says.

"But what happens to our belongings?"

He laughs. "They get wet, too."

I realize I can't stoke concern where there is none, so I stop asking questions.

Upon our arrival, we go to the canoe rental office, where the woman not only charges us thirty-eight dollars to risk our lives but also insists that we sign a hold-harmless waiver, relinquishing them from any liability for our bad judgment.

"It's early in the season and the river is high, but the water's still within the riverbanks," the woman says.

Well, how lucky can we be? I have the urge to say. I hadn't even thought of the possibility of a flood. She warns of the fast-paced current, fallen trees, and other assorted debris around which we will need to navigate with help from the river patrol. The words "fallen trees," "debris," and "river patrol" clog my mind. I'm now convinced I will battle the evils of the underworld, but unlike Beowulf, Gilgamesh, and Dante, I will not emerge a better person for it.

My anxiety level subsides a bit when I see the orange life vests. The color is fitting, I think, seeing as I'm a prisoner on the river for the day.

After realizing I'm the only adult holding a vest, I say, "You can't be too safe, you know."

"Good idea," Michael says.

I examine it with hesitation. "Has this been washed?"

"You mean this year?"

"I take that as a no."

We board an old, rickety bus that once passed inspection for the safe transport of children to school. Now, it hauls half-crocked adults to the river's edge. I eye the bus driver with suspicion after noting the colored sketch of two frothy beer mugs posted above the rearview mirror. Everything will be fine, I assure myself, while a nearby cattle dog sits on his owner's lap, eagerly waiting for the bus to pull out. Obviously, the dog has done this before. I'm jealous that his doggie life vest complements his fur. "Isn't that cute?" people say as they pass the dog. They fail to acknowledge an orange vest on a middle-aged woman.

As we travel down Possum Hollow Road, I overhear snippets of conversations about snappers and snakes. I try to distract myself by looking out the windows. Abandoned shanties, rusted-out camper shells, and dilapidated chicken coops remind me that we are far from my comfort zone. I don't know whether to be disappointed or relieved when we make it to the riverbank.

I search for the safest canoe, but I'm not sure what to look for. Perhaps the one without a hole? Michael makes our selection and ties our cooler to the boat with a bungee cord. What if I fall in? I wonder. Why didn't he bring one long enough to secure me to the canoe? Are a sandwich and a bag of chips more important?

He instructs me to sit in the bow, and he sits in the stern, promising to do most of the work. Michael tells me to watch for snags. Snags? I can't admit that I don't know what they are, but I decide these snags are more daunting than, let's say, a sweater snag or a snag in my stockings. Within moments, our canoe nearly topples from my lack of proper attention, and I realize that the snags are nothing short of underwater land mines.

"So how far are we canoeing?" I ask.

"Ten miles," Michael replies.

"Joking, right?"

"No."

"How long will it take?"

"Four to six hours . . . unless we're in a hurry."

I let out a nervous laugh that echoes off the limestone rock formations. I wonder how I will sit like a soldier for that long, since I'm afraid to move the slightest degree to the left or right for fear of tipping the canoe. Settling the best I can, I stare at the dirty water that surrounds me.

"Could have cleaned the place up a bit," I say.

My husband chuckles as we pass a bobbing kitchen chair and a porcelain toilet on the left bank. Pointing to the toilet he says, "Let me know if you need to stop."

There is no way I can admit that I need to use it.

Soon we pass two rafts tied together—twelve women in all. Their hoots and hollers tell me they are here by their own volition. One woman asks the others, "If you could be the opposite sex for the day, what is the first thing you'd do?"

I secretly ponder this question, and my husband eventually asks, "Well, what would you do?"

"Fart in public," I announce, and Michael tells me that life on the river suits me well.

I straighten on the bench, basking in my new image as a river rat, when a strange sound draws my attention. "What was that?" I ask.

Michael points to the riverbank, where a herd of cattle stand both in and out of the water. No wonder the cattle dog needs a life vest. The cows are snorting, moving a little too close to the canoe.

"We're fine," Michael assures me, but for the next few miles, I watch for angry cows, snakes, snappers, wayward fishing lures, and drunken boaters. Just when I decide the dangers on the river are behind us, the sound of thunder erupts.

I look at Michael to gauge his concern. "Hmm," he says, "guess it's time for you to paddle."

Lightning. Aluminum boat. Water. I begin paddling . . . quickly.

Michael has yet to show signs of real concern, which provides some relief. As the wind whips up a cool breeze, the rain pours from the sky, and the lightning crackles overhead, I search for anything that might delay our arrival to the landing. The rain pelts my skin, and the canoe begins taking on water, negating my efforts to keep dry for the past eight miles, and I begin laughing. Michael asks me why I'm laughing, and it suddenly occurs to me that it has been a long time since I let myself go.

"Can't a girl laugh when she's paddling for her life?" I ask.

For the next two miles, the storm worsens and the river rages, but it doesn't matter if we capsize, if a snake slithers on board, or if we're rammed by an angry steer. I realize that I'm having fun and, more importantly, I'm helping to save Nature Boy's life (a story my husband will deny every time I tell it). Salvation soon appears at the takeout landing—the old, rickety bus with the beer-touting driver who will deliver us safely to our car.

Once aboard, Michael glances at the lightning strikes behind us. "That was a little too close."

"Now you tell me," I say.

On the way back, I listen to people brag of cheating danger, and I know I can do the same.

Once home, I relay our harrowing adventure on the Meramec to the children, wherein they reply, "That's nice, Mom. But what's for dinner?"

Michael looks at me and says, "Yeah, what is for dinner?"

"Whatever you decide to make will be fine. I need to book our reservations in the mountains before the cabins fill up."

"We could always use a tent, you know," he suggests.

"Why don't we compromise? A pop-up trailer . . . with a full kitchen."

"Sure."

"Toilet and shower?"

"Absolutely," he assures me.

"Washer and dryer?"

"Uh . . . no."

I sigh. "I suppose I'll survive. Barely."

Michael puts his arm around me and pulls me closer. "I've been thinking . . . How about a little white-water rafting this year?"

—*Cathi LaMarche*

The Piece of Paper
That Almost Blinded Me

I was feeling particularly organized that Friday afternoon. The kids were safely tucked into daycare, and I was plodding along with my daily companion—my To Do list. It was a tattered piece of notebook paper, and in those days, a newly scribbled one accompanied me everywhere I went. With a family wedding in Manhattan in a couple months, I attacked the project of finding the best airfare possible. When satisfied, I proudly e-mailed my husband, David, to let him know what I'd come up with. Surely he'd be happy with my efforts to not take him away from his clients for any longer than necessary.

His response came swiftly and dealt a life-altering message. "We won't make it that long."

Grasping for a reason for my husband's uncharacteristic cruelty, my first thought was that somehow his computer had been taken over by an office prankster. Then I had no choice but to take a long, hard look at my marriage and how we had come to this point in just under seven years.

To be honest, David's e-proclamation shouldn't have come as any big surprise to me. I knew that he and I had drifted apart. Many days, we didn't even feel like friends, let alone lovers. But it was easier for me to chalk it up to the fact that we had two young children, a puppy, a stressful new job for him in a new city, and a new identity (or lack thereof) for me after having worked for sixteen years in an office and now trying to freelance from home and do laundry at the same time. No, we weren't very close these days, but I still had high hopes that things would get better in the future. The problem is, he had no way of knowing that.

He also had no way of knowing that when I feel the first slap of crisp air in the fall, I look forward to watching him watch football. He couldn't know that the mere sound of distant rumblings of a thunderstorm make me wish he was near so we could enjoy whatever comes, together. He didn't know that when I fold his faded yellow, paper-thin, Batman T-shirt, a grin comes over my face simply because I know how much he loves wearing that thing. He never caught me looking out the window while he cuts the grass or read my mind thinking how handsome he still is.

That day, I was flooded with images I simply could not bear—the images of a divorced mother. I tried to imagine unpacking the boxes of Christmas decorations without him. Suddenly, the warm, family ritual seemed like a mere chore to me. I tried to think about coloring Easter eggs without his yearly tradition of pouring all the colors together at the end and brewing up a black one. Still harder to imagine was the early morning ritual of hiding the eggs in the grass, soggy slippers and all, without him by my side. I imagined that the heartache would continue throughout the year. How could packing up the van and eating junk food at the drive-in on the hottest night of the summer be any fun without him to find the perfect parking spot? His passion for Halloween and all things scary made me want to cry at the thought of an October without him.

I tortured myself further and looked around the house at our treasures. Who would take what? We've been married long enough that nearly everything my eyes fell upon didn't say "David" or "Julie," but rather "us." The wedding china with the journal that I use to record every special family meal. The picture of our beloved, late Dalmatian and the matching snow dog that David built next to him in front of our first home together. The house we have now is nice enough, but we've yet to take a drive where we don't pick out a favorite and refer to it as our dream house.

It was something I always just assumed we'd end up in.

David travels a lot on business, and I don't think I've ever told him that when he's gone, I don't feel like we're much of a family. We're two kids, a puppy, and a crazed mom who play, eat, take baths, and go to bed. When he's home, we play, eat, take baths, and go to bed, but it's somehow more meaningful when we're doing it all together.

In the flurry of doctors' appointments, vet appointments, swim lessons, tennis lessons, ballet lessons, I'd failed to notice something. In my insistence that we visit amusement parks, take extended family vacations, line up sitters for parties with our friends, and host an array of dinners, I failed to notice something. Picking up his dry cleaning and making sure we always have stadium mustard and Entenmann's raspberry crumb cake is not enough. Loving David's devilish grin on my daughter's face and unending curiosity in my son are not enough. I need to love David with the same amount of enthusiasm that I do everything else.

I'm not ignorant. I catch *Oprah* on occasion and read articles in women's magazines. I'm aware that marriages often fall apart under the guise of family life. I've read how taking care of yourself is the best thing you can do for your family. In fact, last year for my birthday, we all laughed as I declared it "The Year of Julie." After five years of either being pregnant or nursing, I shed my motherhood hormones and tried to find a glimmer of my old self under the antibacterial haze. I gouged out time for walking again. I stacked books about anything but mothering high on my bedside table. I attacked my writing with energy I didn't even know I still had. Only now do I see that, along the way, I'd expected my marriage to survive on fumes.

The phrase "reconnecting with your partner" is everywhere, and suddenly I know what it means.

I dug out my favorite old picture of David and me when we first started dating and put it in a new frame on our dresser. I remember so clearly the day it was taken. I knew that he was the perfect mate for me; it's written all over my wrinkle-free face. How could I have let that awareness become so hidden over the years? I'm wearing his shirts around the house again as a Lagerfeld-scented reminder to myself that my man—not my kids' daddy—sleeps next to me at night. We traded vehicles this past weekend because mine gave him more room for the guys' annual camping trip. Just driving his SUV even made me feel closer to him. And I'm just getting started.

Although I'd have appreciated a little warning along the way, I know that David handled his frustration the best way he could. He silently, then not so silently, brooded about his lack of presence in my life until he couldn't take it. He simply couldn't feel like the last thing on my To Do list any longer. It was shocking to me because in my mind, he never was at the bottom. He's always right up there at the top. Sadly, though, I'm not sure I realized that until I was forced to look at it. When I did, I was happy to discover that every daydream I have involves David and me, in some far-away land, exploring together. My dream companion wasn't necessarily my friends or my family, the people with whom I share my daily thoughts, nor even my kids, who get every ounce of my love day in and day out; it was my husband, David.

I heard somewhere that the best thing a father can do for his children is to love their mother. The TV must've been on at the time, and I probably said, "Aw, that's nice," and kept on with my list-making. After my wake-up call and resulting mental inventory, though, I now realize that not only is loving David the best thing I can do for my children, it's also the best thing I can do for myself. And even if his name is not always scribbled on that piece of paper I carry around with me, he's always at the top of my list.

—*Julie Clark Robinson*

Lime Green and Not Deep

I dated Jim for six months. The relationship was comfortable, probably because deep down I knew it wasn't going anywhere. There was no chemistry and, therefore, no risk. When we finally slept together, it was exactly as expected—nice, pleasant, fine. That is, until two weeks later when he trotted out the video. Okay—I admit to being just a tad stupid. I mean, I knew he was a private investigator and I saw the camera pointed at the bed. It simply never occurred to me that it was on.

So once the video was safely overwritten by *Peggy Sue Got Married*, it was back to the drawing board—going to singles parties and experimenting with personal ads. It wasn't long before I met another guy named, you guessed it, Jim. He told me he had never, ever had a second date. Without going into great detail, let's just say that I discovered, firsthand on our first date, myriad reasons why this may, in fact, have been true. I suspect he eventually purchased a Russian bride, who no doubt dumped him as soon as her papers were in order. And he undoubtedly had it coming.

I finally surrendered to destiny and gave the dating thing a much-needed rest.

I joined an upscale health club with my friend Donna and settled into my new role as a old-spinster-in-the-making. Donna started casually dating a guy she'd met at the club, and after a while I began to secretly hope lightning might strike for me and I'd meet someone extraordinary. But one thing was certain: I would never date another Jim.

So there we were at the club on St. Patrick's Day, 1988. We worked out hard, showered, and headed for the hot tub—I half blind without my glasses and Donna acting as my seeing-eye friend. I remember the water was hot, hot enough to be unpleasant. The place smelled of sweat and chlorine, and it made me vaguely nauseated. Someone slid into the seat across from us—to me, nothing more than a blur. But Donna said, "Hey. I know you. You're . . ."

At this point she cast me a quick sideways glance, then directed her attention back to the guy easing into the hot tub. "You're Gary's roommate."

Gary was the fellow she was dating. Donna had an extensive list of qualifications in future husband material, and Gary met many of her requirements. He had graduated from an Ivy League school, which was high on her list. He also had thick hair. Thick hair was important to Donna because hers was fine and soft, and she figured if she married someone with similar hair, her children would be bald. Because she was short and un-athletic, she wanted to meet someone tall and lanky, with runner's or gymnast's muscles or even football-player muscles. Gary had none of these. He had Pillsbury Doughboy muscles, and this would not do. Hence, the casual relationship.

I was not nearly as picky. I wanted someone who had a job; I didn't care what kind of job. My parents had given significant amounts of cash to both my ex-husband and my subsequent live-in boyfriend, and to my mom's immense relief, I was finally done with rescue missions. Aside from some form of gainful employment, I wanted someone who understood my jokes—someone with a ready smile and a quick wit. And I wanted someone who did not hit, because I had been hit enough.

Gary's roommate looked sweet . . . well, in as much as I could make out his face.

I leaned across the bubbling water, smiled, and offered my hand. "Hi, I'm Nancy."

"Nice to meet you. I'm Jim."

I scurried back to my side of the hot tub. *No bleeping way. Uh-uh. Stay the bleep over there, Jim. At* least, that's what every fiber of my being screamed. Aloud I said, "Pleased to meet you," or something equally polite and noncommittal.

Jim, also without his glasses, squinted nearsightedly at me through the steam, and I think he may have smiled.

My memory of the rest of the evening is vague. Mostly, I remember laughing. Jim was hands-down the funniest guy I had ever met. I was choking with mirth, holding my sides, nearly passing out and drowning in that hot tub. And still the jokes kept coming. Donna was Irish, and it was, as I mentioned, St. Patrick's Day, so we all went to the Ninety Nine restaurant. I laughed so much my stomach was sore for a week. It was as if I'd done a thousand stomach crunches without taking a break. It dawned on me that if I dated Jim I could have magnificent abs while saving a bundle on gym memberships. I gave him my phone number.

And so it began. Every Friday we went to Cambridge to see a comedy show at Catch a Rising Star. Every Tuesday we had dinner with a group of Jim's friends. We watched stupid B movies, and I fell asleep with my head on his shoulder while the silver screen ingénues in *Barbarella* or *The Perils of Gwendolyn in the Land of the Yik Yak* jiggled their way across the screen.

He invited me to his house, where Gary slept in a king-sized bed in the master bedroom and Jim slept on a twin mattress on the floor of a tiny room resembling a closet with windows. Upstairs were two additional bedrooms, both stuffed with Jim's possessions. One was filled with rows and rows of black plastic shelving units from Home Depot, each covered in matching boxes from the post office, neatly stacked and meticulously labeled. The other room had built-in shelves nestled within its walls, and sitting neatly upon each shelf was a stack of folded pants. Every pair of slacks, jeans, and trousers was perfect—each pair crisply ironed and accurately folded to exactly the same length, each stack precisely the same height as the one next to it. And each pants tower was labeled with an identical yellow Post-it, with neatly printed letters that said, "Slightly Tight," "Very Tight," "Very Loose," "Slightly Loose," or "Just Right."

But the pants towers paled next to his yogurt cup collection. These he had amassed for years, and they held a place of honor on a shelf built just for them, immediately adjacent to his plastic bag collection. It was obvious that Jim never parted with anything that might possibly, someday be useful. I suspected this might bode well for a future relationship, as I, too, was useful.

After two failed relationships, I had baggage. I had trust issues. I had been knocked around quite a bit and made to feel even smaller than my five-foot frame might suggest. I trusted no one. I fully expected the relationship to fail, and I figured I would be the one to cause its inevitable demise. It was only a matter of time.

But somehow Jim got past all of that. His first kiss was brushed gently upon my forehead, and I confess that I melted inside. When he invited me to stay over, it was just that—staying over. There was no sex, just cuddling, and I had never felt so completely safe and cherished. When we finally made love, it was the most profound and intensely passionate experience of my life. I know it sounds cliché, but I think maybe we both cried just a little.

Introducing Jim to my family was, well, different. My folks were cleaning out my grandparents' house in Ogunquit, and Jim volunteered to help. He arrived, not dressed to impress his possible future in-laws. No, he wore lime green sweat pants that were undoubtedly taken from the slightly tight pants tower, with a matching lime green sweatshirt that had also seen slimmer days. He had no vanity, no need to impress. He was eternally unguarded, completely open and honest, unapologetically saying, "This is me. This is who I am."

My dad didn't seem to notice Jim's lack of fashion sense. He was too busy checking out the brand new Honda Prelude SI. Out loud, he said, "That's a nice car." But what he meant was, "Thank goodness I don't have to loan him money."

When I met Jim's mom, she turned to him and said, in Italian, "She's no thirty-six, twenty-four, thirty-six, but she has a nice smile."

Jim translated, "She loves your smile." He didn't know I understood Italian.

I remember the question Gary asked when I had been dating Jim for about a week. He looked at me with a completely serious expression and said, "So are you going to marry him?"

A bit taken aback, I replied, "Well, don't you think I should get to know him first?"

Gary laughed dismissively, saying, "What's to know? He isn't very deep."

At the time, his comment seemed insulting. But as the weeks turned into months, I realized Gary was right. Everything I needed to know about Jim was right there on the surface. There was no dark ambush lurking beneath the sweet, geeky façade. He really did wear his heart on his sleeve. And today, after more than two decades of marriage, he is still the very same Jim I met in the hot tub. He still makes me laugh until my stomach hurts, and although the lime-green outfit is (thankfully) long gone, his love for me is so deep it can still make me cry a little.

—Nancy DeMarco

Loving Done Right

I'm back in the city teaching this year, so I get *Raisin* again. I'm so excited.

Just in case that made no sense whatsoever (and unless you're a middle school English teacher, it probably won't), let me clarify: I'm talking about teaching eighth-grade students the play *Raisin in the Sun,* by Lorraine Hansberry. It's a great work of literature, full of wisdom and truth, and I'm hereby ordering everyone who hasn't read it to get a copy now. After reading the play and completing the quizzes and final test, you are allowed to rent the Sidney Poitier movie of the same title. What a treat.

Raisin is a play about racial equality, about lost dreams and hopes that have died, but mostly about love. Not the romantic, falling in and out kind, but the love that lasts—the love that weathers the storms of the years and still survives.

One of the great monologues in the play is given by Mama, Lena Younger. When the family is at its lowest, when her son, Walter Lee, has lost all the money that held the keys to their family's dreams and hopes, his sister, Beneatha, lashes out, calling him a "toothless rat . . . less than a man."

Mama turns to her daughter and says:

". . . Child, when do you think is the time to love somebody the most? When they done good? When they gone and made things easy for everybody? Well, that ain't the time. It's when he's at his lowest, when life done beat him down. When he's at his lowest and can't believe in himself. It's when the world done whipped him."

I remember that speech and how it played a part in the lives of my parents.

To the casual observer, my dad got the lion's share in the marriage stakes, and that's a fact. I've said it before: in Miss Ida, my dad hit a jackpot that would break every casino in Vegas.

He never diapered an infant, nor dressed one, nor picked up after one. He never cleaned a thing in the house. He never cooked a meal. He never washed a load of laundry. When he arose in the morning, a fresh shirt, underwear, overalls (or suit, on Sunday), and socks were laid on the bed waiting. He lived with a wife who never complained, nagged, or bossed. She managed his finances, raised his children, cleaned his house, and cared for his mother and sister, all with a loving nature and kindness that few can match.

She, however, felt she had hit the matrimonial sweepstakes, too. Having one dear sister married to a raging alcoholic with a taste for violence and another married to a man fifty years her senior and browbeaten almost to the breaking point by his domineering family, Ida felt like a princess. Her youngest sister, Celia, married very well: a man of both good character and great intelligence, but "Lord, he carried Celie away from home! All the way to West Virginia, then clear to Omaha, Nebraska." Being more than ten miles from her "good mumma" was a fate Miss Ida couldn't begin to fathom.

So she considered herself dead lucky. Always did. Archie Clements worked hard, was a good father, a good role model, got himself up for church on Sunday, never drank. He was a responsible man, a civic leader, a man of respect in the community. And he paid attention to her. When it came to making a business deal, A.B. had the good sense to listen to his wife. She was his partner and equal when it came to finance. (She was actually his superior, but let's give Dad his due, shall we?) Together, they achieved the two great dreams of her life: a nice brick home and a college education for their two children. And in his own way, Dad let her know she was valued, loved, and appreciated. It wasn't with candy, flowers, and diamonds, but those things weren't what Miss Ida was all about.

In both of their minds, Dad did his part. He worked like a dog. Miss Ida was eleven years his junior; she'd outlive him by twenty years, at least. He worked every day, mindful that she'd need enough to get by when he was gone. The men of my father's generation "dropped like flies," as he put it, of heart attacks and cancer. He buried his friends and acquaintances—and kept working, knowing he'd never outlive Miss Ida.

Fate stepped in, however, to confound Dad's common sense. At age seventy-two, Miss Ida developed cancer. And damn that disease straight to the lowest depths of hell. I try to hate no one in this world. But I harbor a hatred of cancer that borders on fanatical. No single man, however evil his soul, could ever inflict such slow, racking pain on others. No man would have the patience to torture that way, to take away coordination, then mobility, then speech, then sight, then mental capacity, then finally, finally, the entire body itself, over the course of months and months.

And Dad stepped to the plate, as it were. Only the best; forget the cost. He cared for a father, a mother, and a sister until their last breath. Miss Ida would get the same . . . No, she'd get better treatment.

She was told she could try chemotherapy. She could go to the Medical College of Virginia, an hour's drive away, and have the treatments three times a week. It might help lengthen her life. Here's a secret Dad doesn't know: she didn't want to. She wanted to go home to the Lord. He was waiting there for her, no doubt about it. But Lord, Archie. What would he do? If she could "tough it out," maybe she could take care of him a few more years. She had to try, any road. Miss Ida was a fighter, she was. She fought through cancer in her sinus cavity and through cancer in her colon, but the disease finally had its way, three years later, in the hideous form of a brain tumor.

But back to the original chemotherapy. Who in the world would take her to the treatments? I was teaching in Lynchburg, three hours away. Moses, my brother, was the county engineer, working ten hours a day and rearing his own two boys. How would Ida get to MCV every Monday, Wednesday, and Friday?

"Well, Good Lord, I'll get in the car and take her," responded Archie. "Reckon I still have enough sense to drive to Richmond, any road."

Well, Moses looked at me and I looked at him. No words were spoken, but the question hung between us. Who's going to tell Dad he's too old to drive Interstate 95 to Richmond? Being a soul who has always felt discretion to be the better part of valor, I flat out refused to open my mouth; Moses, having a bit more courage, had the gumption to say, "Dad, uh . . . do you think . . ." before getting an Archie Clements "wither you straight down to the floor" glare. Then he shut up too.

Anyway, the American Cancer Society saved us from the horns of that dilemma, and God bless them for it. Seems they had a van for Southside, Virginia, that would take Miss Ida right from her door to MCV, and back again, every treatment. Guess who went with her? You got it: A.B., complaining about how fast the driver was going—"He'll kill us all before it's said and done!"—every mile of the way. The man who hated to stir five miles from his door washed up, put on a suit and tie, and went to Richmond three days a week, for six weeks, at the age of eighty-six. Just to be there for Miss Ida. Just to hold her hand and keep her company.

And when it got bad, got really, really bad, terminal brain-tumor bad, he didn't quaver. Brain tumor; no hope. Well, fine. We'll need round-the-clock nurses; who can you recommend? Not for a second did he consider any alternative. Nursing home? Forget it. Miss Ida was going to be in the place she loved most: home. Home and safe. Happy as he could make her.

Eight months. That's right. Eight months. Nurses, round the clock for eight months. That's what she needed. That's what she got. The man who saved every penny he ever made, who drove one particular truck for twenty-two years before it literally fell apart, threw open his wallet. Wide.

And every night, through it all, he walked into their bedroom. (He had long since evacuated to my old room, but he went in at bedtime, nonetheless.) Held her hand and told her, "I love you, Miss Ida. Good night. I'm a right lucky man to have you for a wife."

Cost him a king's ransom. He lived with the stench of diapers, of vomit, of death, for eight months. Lived with strangers tracking in and out of his house. He's a very private man, and he hated it all. But every night, he walked in that room, he put a smile on that face, and he told her, "I love you, Miss Ida. I'm lucky I found you."

He was, of course. Lucky. She would have done the same for him in half a heartbeat. But how many would stick? How many would give that "full measure of devotion," as Mr. Lincoln called it? I wonder.

Miss Ida and A.B. knew what Lena Younger knew. They knew about loving when someone is down, about giving when a person needs it most, without question, without reservation, without thinking of what's in it for you.

And here's what I always tell my eighth-grade students. Go out, find someone you love. Then picture them old, bald, sick, costing you a fortune both emotionally and financially. Ask yourself: *Will I still be able to say "I love you?" Will I still say "I'm lucky I found you?"*

If the answer is no, keep looking. If it's yes, run for the altar as quickly as you can, for those relationships come but once in many, many lifetimes.

—*Connie Ellison*

My Year in China

In my house I don't need a calendar to chart the passage of time. I can plot the years more simply, by my husband's passions. 2009: The Year of the China Obsession.

Several months ago, Marc decided he wanted to read ancient Chinese classics—and any old translations wouldn't do. He cruised the Internet, compiling a master reading list from the websites of the major universities offering courses in Chinese studies—Harvard, Princeton, the University of Chicago. Then he tracked down the books through Amazon.com and wrote himself a syllabus. Now, more than thirty books are piled on his bedside table, a tower of books, his own personal Great Wall of China: such classics as *The Three Kingdoms*; the six-volume *The Dream of the Red Chamber*, also inexplicably known as the *Story of the Stone*; Anthony C. Yu's *Journey to the West* (in four different volumes); the *Analects of Confucius*; the *I Ching*; a history of daily life in China on the eve of the Mongol Invasion (thirteenth century, in case you care); assorted myths and legends; and my personal favorite, *China's Examination Hell: Civil Service Exams of Imperialist China*. The more arcane, the better.

"This stuff reads like a Chinese *Peyton Place!*" he says, eyes alight, as he plows through *The Plum in the Golden Vase*.

He particularly savors the footnotes. "Do you want to know about the system of keeping concubines?" he'll ask. "And did you know they use the patronymic as a first name?"

My eyes glaze over.

Marc talks about teaching himself to read Chinese: a character a day. "In ten years, I'd know almost four-thousand characters," he says.

And I may not be one of them, I think, but smile instead.

The smile gets a little forced, though, when he starts downloading Chinese fonts for his computer; and when he does a Google search on the subject of "tea" and hyperlinks into Hong Kong, where he learns how to prepare tea in the traditional Chinese way; and when the tea catalogs arrive followed by mail orders of $100 worth of loose tea leaves, as well as a traditional covered Chinese tea cup from which to drink it.

In self-defense, I flee the house for a cappuccino at Starbucks, only to turn on the CD player in his car and be assaulted by the sound of Chinese pipa music.

Whenever there is a lull in our conversation, he reverts to the subject of his passion. And so it goes: the winter of his Chinese content.

This love affair with China is not new. It may, in fact, be genetic. His father was stationed in China during World War II, an eighteen-year-old from Brooklyn who returned with a pocket full of ancient Chinese coins and a brown scrapbook of photos of his nude Chinese girlfriend.

"Just think," Marc says, "somewhere in China I may have a half-brother."

In high school, he talked about majoring in Chinese, until his mother sat him down. "Honey," she said, "you can't even pass high school Spanish."

So what's a wife to do when her husband's passion bores her silly?

Well, I overstate. It's not the interest I mind; it's the total immersion—the depth, the breadth, the sheer, one-track mindedness of it all. Often, when there is a lull in our conversation, he'll get that far-away look, an air of distraction, but at least I never have to worry he's thinking of another woman. Oh no. More likely, he's pondering the genealogy of the Ming dynasty.

"What are you thinking about?" I'll say.

Sheepishly, he'll say, "You don't really want to know."

I never laugh. Out loud. Oh, I may roll my eyes once in a while, but a wife's got to have a little room to react. Besides, I know we won't be in China forever.

Because last year we went to outer space: The Cosmos. The Final Frontier. 2008 was The Year of the Telescope. Astronomy was the reigning passion. Not just a subscription to *Sky & Telescope*, mind you. It was a full-blown love affair with the stars.

He downloaded star maps from NASA. He trudged the whole family across a frozen field in the dead of winter to watch a comet we could easily see from our own back yard. He drove to the mountains of rural Pennsylvania to track down one of the country's experts on configuring telescopes, boned up on all the optics involved, determined which scope he could couple with a camera in order to do some astral photography, and finally, after an endless one-sided discussion, ordered a telescope. His only regret: that we had neither space nor money for the twelve-incher he really wanted.

Then we needed a vehicle to transport the thing, so we traded in our car (well, actually, the lease was up) for a station wagon, not because I'm a June Cleaver wannabe but because, as Marc happily pointed out, we could take the telescope on family vacations, like some bulky third child.

Currently, the telescope sits in a very large, customized, padded suitcase in the corner of our bedroom, where the five-year-old has to be dissuaded from climbing on it.

And the passion before that? I like to think of that as The Year of the Rowing Machine, where every night I would listen to him recount how many meters he'd rowed, watch him faithfully record them on the spreadsheet he set up on the computer, hear again and again how close he was to the 10 million-meter mark. Every night at 10:30, you'd find him in the basement, lashed to the machine like Ben-Hur, the TV turned up way too loud so he could hear it over the rhythmic sound of the rowing machine that breathes like bellows, a metallic lung whirring *shuuuush, shuuuush*.

And so I chart the passage of our lives together: The Year of Arctic Exploration. The Year of Arthurian Romance. The Year of Glacial Geology. The Year of Fractals and Chaos Theory. The Year of Kafka.

Yes, Franz. It began innocently, with our hand-in-hand stroll through an exhibit of Kafka photos and memorabilia at the Jewish Museum, then progressed to full-blown purchasing madness: Every book Kafka ever penned. All the Kafka biographies. Photo essays on Prague. Kafka's letters. Kafka's friends' letters. You get the idea.

So what will next year bring? Ancient Sumerian texts? Thermal oceanography? Conversational Urdu? The Monkey chants of New Guinea?

Marc offers a clue. "When I'm done with China, I think I'll do India," he says.

Uh-oh. Time for chicken vindaloo. Break out the Ravi Shankar records.

"Now, don't laugh," he'll say, and I know I'm about to hear about a new passion.

"Thank you for not making fun of me," he'll say. "Thank you for listening."

All right, so now I feel a little guilty. But even though the interests are not ones I always share, I do love that he's so totally taken over by them. He brings this passion, this intensity, to everything: to me, our marriage, our children, his work. This was the intensity that first drew me in.

"We're going too fast," I said to him on our second date, pulling out of a long kiss. "I think we should put the brakes on a little."

"We can put on the physical brakes," he said readily. "But please don't put on the emotional ones."

That just about did me in. A man who wasn't afraid to feel, to admit he felt, who welcomed intimacy? I was hooked.

On the day of our wedding, finally alone in the car, Marc lifted my hand and kissed it. "My dad would have loved you," he said.

It made me well up.

The year after Marc's dad died was The Year of the Ham Radio. Nightly, he listened to Radio Havana (in English) and fired off postcards to Cuba.

"If life is as good there as you keep saying, how come everyone is trying to leave?" he'd write.

That was the 1960s, the time of the Cold War and the Cultural Revolution, but still he wrote away to Radio Havana as well as Radio Beijing, probably the only kid in America who was regularly receiving brown paper bundles from China filled with Maoist pamphlets, which made his mother a little hysterical. "Stop it! The FBI will be after you," she'd say. I picture my husband as a skinny little boy, looking much like my sons: blue-eyed, long lashed, and trusting, smelling sweetly of milk and mud. And I ache for that boy who lost his father too soon.

This is a man who will never be bored and never be boring. This is a man who could retire tomorrow and find forty things to do. And this is what first drew me to him—the insatiable intellectual curiosity. That and the kissing.

"When we retire, we should move to a college town," he says. "Forget Florida. Cultural wasteland. It's the land of the Early Bird Special."

Life with him is not dull. He makes me laugh. This is a man who, when an old boyfriend called me after seventeen years of silence, simply handed me the phone and said, "It's for you. It's Charlie." No questions.

He's the guy my parents called whenever there was a medical emergency. How many times did he carry my mother to the emergency room in the middle of the night and sit by her stretcher, insisting she be seen, and attended to, immediately? He's comfortable, and comforting, in hospitals. Thirty years ago he ran the admitting desk at the University of Chicago Medical Center. Well, what else does a person do with a master's degree in medieval and Renaissance literature?

And this is the same guy who held my hand in the labor room when I yelled, "Lamaze, shlamaze, get me *drugs!*" Although he did do one unforgivable thing: somewhere around 4:00 A.M., he put his head down on the foot of my gurney and passed out. And had the nerve to snore. But when our first son was born and roomed in with me and I recovered from the long labor and C-section, Marc stayed in the hospital too, jumping up from the cot every time the baby snuffled or sighed. And he held our infant son and crooned to him so gently that I felt weepy with love and forgave him—mostly—for falling asleep in the labor room.

So what do you do if the passion of the moment, the flavor of the month, the obsession of the year leaves you cold?

You listen. Because you know that were it reversed, he would listen to you. Because you realize that he doesn't drink, gamble, smoke, or womanize, and that you always know exactly where he is. Because he's your best friend, lover, and companion, the guy who in the aftershock of an early morning earthquake could still turn to you in bed and ask, "Did the earth move for you too?"

So bring on the garam masala and the *Bhagavad Gita*, and to India I will go. Because you know what? I wouldn't miss any of his adventures. Not for all the tea in China.

—*Liane Kupferberg Carter*

The Prism

"Hon, you look naked in that swimsuit." My husband's voice curls into my ear. His nose is in my hair, his hands on my waist. Our baby is sandwiched between us, tiny swim trunks riding so high on his pear-shaped body that he looks like a mini-Florida retiree. My husband's tone is one part possessive and one part flirtatious. His voice competes with the echoes of splashes and squeals bouncing off the tiled surfaces of the indoor water park. The air is thick with chlorine and humidity. I smile, thinking I know what he means but am not exactly sure.

We are on a family weekend getaway at a water-park hotel in the suburbs, an hour's drive from our Chicago home. Our five-year-old daughter run-walks (running is prohibited) a circuit within the kiddie section, sliding from one small waterslide to the next.

Her brown skin gleams over her equine spine; she is lean and long. There was never a moment of chubbiness in her babyhood. She is unlike her baby brother, whose thick white thighs grip my hip like a vice.

When my daughter was growing inside me, unborn, my husband was not jealous of me, would not have cared if I looked naked in my swimsuit. That was a time, too, when I probably would not have gone on a suburban weekend water-park trip, thinking it was not cultured or quaint or perfect enough.

After my husband's swimsuit comment, I hoist the baby into his arms so I can go to the bathroom. I make my way past the wet swirling slides, over a faux bridge with a rope railing spanning the "lazy river," to the women's locker room. There, I peek in the mirror.

My swimsuit is white, and I am afraid what my husband meant is that you can see the color of my flesh and the bulges of my post-partum belly through it. But the swimsuit is lined and my fears are not realized. Though wet, the swimsuit still appears white, not transparent. Its dress-like shape floats away from my belly and does not cling. I found it featured in a magazine article about swimsuits designed to hide the flaws of a "mom" figure.

The water park is filled with teenage and twenty-something girls in micro bikinis and with round breasts and taut bellies. In the presence of these girls, the idea that my mom swimsuit is erotic to anyone strikes me as amusing. That it is erotic to my husband is reassuring.

While the swimsuit is not clinging and not transparent, I see the outline of my nipples. This probably inspired my husband's "naked" comment. It does not bother me, though it once may have made me self-conscious. I am still nursing the baby and my breasts feel about as erotic to me as my arms. In the bevy of half-naked younger girls, I feel inconspicuous enough.

When I met my husband in college, he would lope around campus like a bouncing question mark, no taller than I, his posture a curve, skinny inside his baggy clothes. He was always quick to ingratiate himself with others, which I thought of as kindness and gentleness. I never saw him lose his temper. He seemed so nonthreatening, a guy who would not, could not, hurt me. I understand now why harmlessness appealed to me. My dad had spent years drilling the mantra "boys only want one thing" into my head; my mom was afraid for me to walk anywhere outside alone, day or night, lest I get abducted; and college campuses were rife with seminars on date rape and domestic violence. Though I had experienced none of those things, their threats breathed down my neck.

But there was more to my future husband than a mild temperament. The first time I met him, with a girlfriend of mine, he leaned against his dorm-room bunk bed and pronounced to us, "Yeah, I'm a virgin." (We had not asked.) "I think that's cool," he added.

He was a freshman then, and I was a slightly more experienced sophomore, so I raised my eyebrows and smirked. Secretly, though, I admired his courage in putting it out there.

His folks pressured him relentlessly to become a doctor, so he started out pre-med. But in art classes he found expression painting cartoon-like characters oozing color, humor, and vulnerability. When he switched his major to art, he received no end of grief from his parents. But he stuck to his guns. So I began to see him as a person willing to be himself— his goofy, creative, vulnerable self—no matter what others thought. And that is what attracted me.

He and I started dating my senior year. After five years we got married in a white-steepled country chapel with artful black and white photos to prove it.

But he and I looked mismatched. Commuting on the train together to our separate jobs with different dress codes, I would be in a blouse and slacks, he in a T-shirt and jeans. I looked like the grownup, he the kid. People often seemed to think we were not a couple. Sometimes they walked right between us. At a fast-food restaurant, I would have to interject, "I'm with him," even though he had just ordered for both of us.

At home, if the furnace broke, I was the one to call for repairs. I was the one to find the best deal, show the workers what to do, argue when the work was not done right. He was afraid to offend, to make demands.

Before our daughter was born, we were at a party with a girlfriend of mine. My husband sat off to the side as my friend and I chatted. Two guys approached us, drinks in hand, and began to chat. They were bores. It was clear they thought I was single. I threw a "rescue me" look to my husband. I did not expect him to make threats or start a fight. I thought he would come stand beside me, put his arm around my waist, give the nonverbal "back off" cues. He did nothing but smirk, amused at my predicament.

During this time period I got pregnant, accidentally. There was a miscarriage, then a difference of reactions. I was bereft; he was relieved. A year later, he reluctantly agreed to a second pregnancy. I became pregnant with our daughter. But during that year, things changed. He had stopped looking at me.

He had stopped ogling me in his trademark adolescent way. He would walk out of a room I was in and turn out the light, forgetting I was there.

It continued this way until our daughter was two years old. One night he and I were lying in bed together. He was facing the wall, and I was stretched out next to him looking at the back of his head. He had talked a lot about a woman at work when I was pregnant, then not at all afterward.

"Don't worry, she's married," he had said. "She's just a friend."

I had not wanted to ask about her this night, but I knew I had to.

I was surprised to hear of the woman's divorce and her new boyfriend. I had not known everything then, so I am not sure how I knew to ask, but I did. "Are you jealous of her new boyfriend?"

He whispered to the wall, "I think so."

I attempt one of the adult water slides while my husband holds the baby. Moving in line step by step up a wet staircase to the top of the slide, the outside landscape slowly reveals itself through the tall windows. A solid rain falls into a pond with ducks, circled by prairie grass. It is calm and scenic. But the higher I move, the more I see. The pond is tucked into the elbow of a highway on-ramp, where cars glide past construction equipment, piles of dirt, and a dump truck.

The water slides protrude outside of the building from the top and curl back inside at the ground level, like plastic noodles dripping rain onto the concrete below. Inside the building, I hurl myself down the dark plastic tube, where I get twirled and twisted and dropped.

One night in the weeks after discovering the affair I was driving home from a far suburb with my daughter. She was two years old. Snow blanketed street signs on the unlit road so I could not tell where I was going. Visions of my husband and the other woman tumbled over and over in my brain.

My daughter began to whimper. Strapped into her car seat behind me, she wanted out. But I could not stop the car. It was too dark, the streets too isolated.

Another vision of my husband and the woman accosted me. A tangle of arms, legs, and . . . *Stop! Stop! Stop!* I silently admonished myself, repeatedly, futilely. I could not stop my torturous thoughts. My skin crawled. My daughter started screaming. I fought a rising panic.

I made a wrong turn, then another. I could not catch my breath. As I approached a railroad track, I saw the train and had a flash—just a flash—of a vision of me driving the two of us into it.

At the bottom of the waterslide, I slosh around in the catch pool, where it is bright and noisy and exuberant. I see my husband standing on the side, waiting, watching, smiling. The baby is balanced on his hip; our daughter is holding his hand. "There's Mom!" he says to her. He is looking at, not past, me. His stance is wide, his feet anchored, his shoulders broad.

Together, we make our way to a lukewarm hot tub, lit turquoise from below.

We worked to recover our marriage. We went to counseling once a week. We read books about affairs. We looked at the patterns of our behavior and deliberately changed them.

There was no magic moment when I said, "I am so in love with you that I forgive you." There was no scene where he ran after me in slow motion with a fistful of wildflowers. His affair was like a fulcrum in our lives, a prism where the light comes in imperceptibly and comes out split, defined, divided into its separate parts.

Over the course of several months, he became more like a grownup. And I became less of one.

The next day when we are leaving the hotel, the sky is a steel drizzle. I stand outside with the kids waiting for my husband to get the car. A balding man in a sleeveless shirt is smoking nearby. He is shivering, hugging himself against the chill. My husband pulls our car up to the curb. As I am about to get in, the guy suddenly becomes animated. He makes conversation with me about the model of our car, a battered station wagon. I wonder about the guy's enthusiasm.

Once I am in the car, my husband says, "That guy's a creep. I saw him lurking around the hot tub."

"Hmmph," I say as we drive away.

Later that night, at home with the kids asleep, my husband and I sneak into our bedroom to do what we had not been able to do with the kids in the hotel room: make love. With his arms around me and his skin warm, he says again, "You looked naked in that swimsuit," with a smile.

"What do you mean naked? It wasn't like you could see through the fabric," I say.

"But I could see the outline of your nipples," he explains. "And that guy was looking at you in the hot tub."

"Oh, the 'creep!'"

I nestle into the normalcy of his jealousy, his irritation, his desire to hold me and make love to me and find me sexy in a mom swimsuit.

—*Stephanie Springsteen*

A Gift for Women

I was about to walk around the side of our house, but stopped when I heard my husband, Eric, talking to our neighbor's sixteen-year-old son.

"Women are not like us," he said. "And nowhere is that more clear than when you have to buy them a gift. Forget logic and practicality, and think useless and a waste of money."

"I don't even know why she gave me a present, it's not my birthday!" young Steve pointed out.

"That's the whole point! They only give you things because then you have to buy them something back. They don't limit themselves to rational events, like birthdays and Christmas. They dream up anniversaries, like the day we first kissed and the first time you said you loved me. Most of the time, you won't remember any of these things, but there is nothing you can do to stop them," Eric said in his "expert" voice.

With my own birthday coming up, I smiled and kept listening.

"My father once gave my mother an electric blanket. They had no central heating, and their bed was always freezing. Did she appreciate a suitable present like that? Of course not! She would have preferred a bunch of roses, a great asset when your feet are freezing all night long!" I could tell Eric was well into his subject now and enjoying himself.

"Well, I was going to get Carrie a book token because she has to pay a fortune for a lot of her study books," young Steve ventured.

"A book token," Eric repeated in a voice close to alarm. "Don't even think about it! Any book is a pretty risky thing to buy them. They might love cooking, but if you give them a book on it, they will take it as a criticism of their cooking. They can be into a particular sport, but they don't want to read a book on how to improve at it."

"So what kind of book can you buy then?" Steven asked.

"Some rubbish on their secret heartthrob, like how George Clooney came to be an actor or David Beckham's views on women's fashion. I would just forget a book; it's too risky," Eric advised.

"You are still thinking logically," he went on. "You said Carrie shares a flat with some friends and it costs a fortune for electricity as they study into the early hours. Now, we might think a decent reading light with one of those new 'eco' bulbs that burns forever would be a good idea. But no! A woman would rather have a multicolored candle that gives off the scent of lotus blossoms and as much light as the moon on a cloudy night!"

I heard Steve laugh. "Her mum gave Carrie one of those for her birthday, and she loved it. You are spot on, Mr. Stark!"

"Perfume never goes wrong. They aren't happy until they have a row of bottles of all shapes and sizes," Eric offered. "The thing to do is pick something with the name of someone famous in a really fancy bottle. It is not so much the using of it but the showing it off to friends that pleases them. You can always say you chose it because you think it is very seductive; they like that even more."

"Jewelry is probably the best bet; it's the most useless thing around. Try to see what kind of things she wears. The best thing is to say, 'I just felt like it was you!' It panders to their egos, and they will love it even though they hate it."

Eric went on with his sage advice. "Whatever you choose, you have to remember the wrapping. Wrapping is absolutely one of the most important issues when buying gifts for a woman. It is best to find one of those shops that will do the wrapping for you; if not, then get your sister to help. You need whatever new shiny paper they like at the moment and one of those totally useless rosette things that matches. If you can get coils of stuff to stick on as well, you are home and dry before they even open it."

"I am so glad I spoke to you; you really know women," Steve said.

I went back into the house and studied a number of things that Eric had given me for birthdays and anniversaries. Perfumes named after famous stars in weird-shaped bottles, a book about Tom Cruise, and three different earring and pendant sets in my favorite colors of red and purple. I smiled as a plan came to me.

The next day I casually said to my husband, "I am going along to Donna's church sale. I have a number of nice things I can donate."

"What kind of things?" Eric asked.

"Oh, perfumes; I can never go through them all. And some books I have read. And some of my jewelry; I can only wear so much. We don't go out much these days, so I don't have the same call for these things."

I could see Eric visibly taking stock; that ruled out three of his first choices for my upcoming birthday.

On my birthday morning, I went down to breakfast, prepared by Eric, who was waiting for me at the table. I found a card sitting at my place and next to it another little envelope tied up with red ribbon. I opened the smaller envelope carefully. It read: "Confirmation of dinner for two at The Old Castle Restaurant."

I looked up at Eric, eagerly watching me. I beamed at him. Old Castle was the best restaurant in the whole area, small and romantic, with a coal fire burning in the corner and candles on the table. "It's fantastic! What on earth made you think of that?" I asked him.

"Oh, well, I thought it would give you a chance to wear your fancy perfumes and your jewelry," he said. "I'm not daft; I recognize a hint when I get one."

As I got up and went into his arms to hug him, I smiled to myself. It was never meant as a hint to go out somewhere, but I'd never tell him that.

His views on women probably had some truth in them; it was the all-knowing tone that had annoyed me. On the other hand, I knew that Eric did not particularly like having meals out; he just wanted to please me. He had missed out on the most important point for Steve: Everything he gave me was out of love, and that's what made the gifts special. That's what made me love him so much.

—*Joyce Stark*

The First Thing about Love

"Love? . . . She didn't know the first thing about love!"

This scornful verdict from Ira, in the novel *Breathing Lessons*, by Anne Tyler, is aimed at his son Jesse and at Fiona, the teenage mother of Jesse's child. Ira's timid wife, Maggie, would love nothing more than to see her son happily married, and she desperately wants a relationship with her granddaughter. She contends that Jesse and Fiona still love each other and that love can prevail over their messy history. Ira's contemptuous response leaves Maggie perplexed.

She asks hesitantly, "What is the first thing about love?"

Good question. In its early stages, my relationship with the love of my life certainly appeared less than promising.

We met during a training session for a theater company in Los Angeles, California. I had been in a rehearsal until 4:00 A.M. and was comatose on the floor of a classroom. That is, until I was rudely awakened at the crack of dawn by the sound of some completely insensitive, and apparently blind, Canadian hick singing a twangy folk song at the top of his lungs and strumming his guitar with great gusto.

Hello? I thought. *Can this moron not see that I'm sleeping here?*

That was our introduction. If someone would have told me then that this would be the man I would marry and with whom I would create two amazing little individuals, I probably would have asked them to suffocate me with my own pillow then and there. For one thing, at that first meeting, I was wearing a large diamond ring from someone else. Someone different, very different, from Calvin.

Michael, my fiancé at the time, was in medical school. Let me just say now that the qualities that make a great doctor aren't always as appealing in a romantic partner. I've always believed that a man's closet defines him. Michael's closet was a three-sided walk-in affair. The left side was all shirts, from his most casual T-shirt to his most highly starched and properly labeled dress shirt, all on brown plastic hangers arranged in a precise order, one inch apart. Straight ahead were pants—

jeans to khakis to suit trousers—all stiffly creased, also on brown plastic hangers, exactly one inch apart. Jackets were to the right. Shoes were on the floor in plastic boxes, computer labeled, and in order from athletic shoes to dress shoes.

I once left a wet towel on the floor at Michael's apartment for a minute or two while I dried my hair, and the incident nearly became a deal-breaker. I once helped him hang a Van Gogh print over his dresser. It took us an hour and a half, the use of two tape measures and a level, and the need to rearrange the two items on the dresser sixty-four times to create the right visual effect. I'm actually surprised that Michael liked Van Gogh, Vincent being such an artistically and emotionally messy guy.

Calvin's closet was . . . well, not even a closet. It was a suitcase. A suitcase from Goodwill with a broken handle held on by duct tape. Inside the suitcase were holey underwear, a couple of T-shirts with the sleeves cut off and printed with some slogan about pickin' and grinnin', and a brown double knit polyester suit, also from Goodwill. His other possessions consisted of a fringed suede jacket, a sleeve garter from which the fabric had disintegrated, a worn Bible, and a guitar named Spanky. He made the curious fashion statement of wearing the sleeve garter with his sleeveless T-shirts.

Out of the more than 150 teams assembled for five-month performance tours to various regions of North America, Calvin and I ended up assigned to the same one. A married couple led our team, which also included another single woman, Gigi. We headed off to wow the Midwest with our dramatic and musical talents, which pleased me greatly since Michael was in his second year of medical school in Illinois.

About two seconds into the tour, Gigi fell madly in love with Calvin. We later learned that this was a habit of hers toward anyone with testosterone and breath in his lungs; actually, breathing was optional. We were all somewhat grateful that she fell for Calvin instead of Lanin, since Lanin was married to Jeannie. But it made things only slightly less complicated because, although I didn't know it then, Calvin promptly fell in love with me. And I, naturally, was in love with Michael. If we could've convinced Michael to fall in love with Gigi, we would've had the perfect square. I know Gigi would've been game.

When I remember that tour, I often picture myself as Rose, in the movie *Titanic*, faced with the choice between the neurotic control freak and the free-spirited drifter. I would get off the phone after a late-night argument with Michael, and there would be Calvin, ready to listen and tell me I'm wonderful and oh-so-misunderstood. There he would be, charming everyone with his guitar, or running everywhere with the eagerness of a puppy, or dropping everything to skip rocks with a five-year-old playmate.

So I—like Rose—returned the big diamond from whence it came and chose the free-spirited drifter in the end.

It took three years to come to that end, during which I went to tour with a performance troupe in Europe, running away from the whole confusing situation. Calvin, undeterred by distance, wrote to me every single day—365 letters. My troupe would arrive at our weekly mail drops, and there would be a mound of letters, all for me. This did not make me particularly popular with the rest of my team, but Calvin's unconditional faithfulness did impress my team leader. She pulled strings to have him sent to Europe. We've often joked that he wore me down with sheer, annoying persistence. In truth, every heart longs to be relentlessly pursued. No one can resist it.

Touring together again, we ended up one afternoon on a mountaintop in Spain. We had crossed the border from France to renew our tourist visas. As we stood gazing over the breathtaking expanse, Calvin got down on one knee and asked me to become his bride. He has since joked that he threatened to jump if I said no, and I have since joked that he threatened to push me off if I said no. There were no actual threats involved. He was my very best friend and my most adventurous playmate. I—again, like *Titanic*'s Rose—was swept away by his beautiful love of life.

Fortunately, unlike Rose's paramour, my rambling, gambling drifter didn't disappear under the waves after a single night of passion. He also lived. And as the song goes, our love went on and on. Long enough for that lack of tidiness and fashion sense to become annoying, for worries about health insurance and mortgages to overshadow the appeal of a free spirit, and for passion to fizzle. After eighteen years of marriage, the "first thing" about love has long disappeared, but these days I'm thinking it's the fourth, tenth, twentieth, or one-hundred-fifty-sixth thing about love that really matters.

I'm certain that had I kept the big diamond, I never would have had to pick up a dirty sock. I'd probably have more spa days and less worry about my bank balance. But I chose the man who never hesitates to cancel an important appointment in order to come home and give me a desperately needed break from the never-ending demands of my two toddlers. He sends me off to Starbucks or Barnes and Noble for the evening while he whips up his specialty of French toast for the kids. I chose the man who rubbed my feet every single night of my pregnancies. The man who still writes me love notes, even when I'm crabby, buys totally impractical presents, and makes a big embarrassing fuss over my little accomplishments. I chose the man who still couldn't care less about what he wears or about making a lot of money, but will drop everything in a nanosecond to hunt bugs or sword-fight or play chess with our son. I chose the man who treats our daughter like a princess, showering her with the same gentle, faithful regard he's always granted me.

The first thing about love.

I, like Maggie, am left wondering what that is.

What I do know for sure is that the true gems of love are not the Heart of the Ocean blue diamond or the big diamond engagement ring. Rather, it's the ring of music and laughter in my home, a man who daily ushers my and my children's wants and needs ahead of his own, and the faithful pursuit of one heart by another.

—*Kristi Hemingway-Weatherall*

Contributors

Tami Absi ("Live, Love, Laugh") is a high school English teacher who resides in Dayton, Ohio. During the last three years of her husband Ron's life, she worked as a freelance writer. Now remarried, she has two children, Jackie and Josh, both of whom are pursuing bachelor's degrees in biology at Ohio University. They take after their father, Tony, the scientist.

Judy L. Adourian ("Come Rain or Come Shine") is the lucky wife of Jean-Marc and proud mother of two sons. Her personal essays have appeared in several publications, including five previous *Cup of Comfort®* anthologies. Judy recently authored "Teaching as a Spiritual Practice," a religious exploration curriculum for which she received a Unitarian Sunday School Society grant.

Annette M. Bower ("The Romance of Ordinary Days") lives, loves, and writes in Regina, Saskatchewan. Her writing appears in anthologies, journals, and magazines in Canada, the United States, and the United Kingdom. She is proud of her three other stories published in the *Cup of Comfort®* series.

Ande Cardwell ("The Taming of the Green-Eyed Monster") writes, paints, and kayaks in Bend, Oregon. She and her enduring husband, John, live in a simple little apartment downtown, a spit above the Deschutes River. Ande makes her living giving babies shots—a tough job, but she's good at it.

Priscilla Carr ("To Love Greatly"), memoirist and poet, has stories published in Adams Media's *Cup of Comfort®* and *Hero* anthology series. Her poetry appears in *Grandmother's Necklace* and *It Has Come to This: Poets of the*

Great Mother Conference. Donald Hall and Robert Bly are her mentors. She is the founder of the Poet's Studio of New Hampshire.

Liane Kupferberg Carter ("My Year in China") lives in New York with her husband and two sons. Her articles and essays have appeared in more than thirty publications, including the *New York Times*, the *Huffington Post*, *Parents*, *Child*, *McCall's*, *Glamour*, *Skirt!*, *Literary Mama*, and *Cosmopolitan*. A 2009 winner of the *Memoir Journal* Prize for Memoir in Prose, she is working on a memoir about raising a child with autism.

Charmian Christie ("Café Amoré") is a freelance writer who specializes in food, gardening, and travel. Her words, recipes, and photos appear in a wide range of magazines, books, and websites. She lives in Ontario with her husband, two cats, and more measuring cups than she cares to admit.

Nancy DeMarco ("Lime Green and Not Deep"), a massage therapist and freelance writer, lives with her husband, Jim, on a mini-farm in rural New Hampshire. They share their home with an ancient guinea pig, two freeloading horses, a flock of chickens, and one psychotic guinea hen. Nancy and Jim are still very much in love.

Michelle L. Devon ("Popcorn Proposal") is a freelance writer and aspiring novelist. The works of Erma Bombeck and Robert Fulghum, with their liberal use of humor sprinkled with poignancy, inspired her to write. Michelle recently traded the desert of West Texas for the humid Gulf Coast beaches near Galveston. She lives and loves there with her two-legged and four-legged family members.

Shawnelle Eliasen ("The Secret of Rugged Terrain") and her husband, Lonny, raise their bevy of boys in Port Byron, Illinois. They live in an old Victorian on the Mississippi River, where Shawnelle home-teaches her youngest sons. Her stories have been printed in *Guideposts*, *Momsense*, *Marriage Partnership*, and anthologies.

Connie Ellison ("Loving Done Right") teaches English at Sandusky Middle School in Lynchburg, Virginia. She lives with her husband, Andrew, and two children, Jean Prince and James Moses, in Elon, Virginia. She is the author of the book *AnyRoad: The Story of a Virginia Tobacco Farm*.

Suzanne Endres ("As Long as Forever") loves to write, read, garden, play with her dogs, goats, and cats, and hang out with her children and grandchildren. She lives in Idaho with her best friend and husband, Alan, in a cabin near HooDoo Mountain. She gets inspiration for stories from her family and pets.

Michele Forsten ("Improv at the Altar"), a college communications director, lives in New York City. Personal essays about her breast cancer experiences have appeared in *Mamm* and *The Advocate* magazines as well as on public radio. She and Barbara were married in Massachusetts in 2008, marking twenty-five years of being a couple. Their ceremony was as unconventional and spontaneous as the Maine event portrayed in this story.

Annette Gendler ("A Room of His Own") lives in Chicago with her husband and three children. Her essays have appeared in *Natural Bridge*, *Bellevue Literary Review*, *Kaleidoscope*, *Under the Sun*, *South Loop Review*, and on flashquake.com. She holds an MFA from Queens University of Charlotte, and teaches memoir writing and English composition. She also does public relations and advertising for her children's school.

Ariella Golani ("Matchmaker") and her family live in New England. A graduate of Barnard College, Columbia University, she attended the Hebrew University as a visiting scholar and holds a JD from the University of Michigan Law School. She has completed her first novel and is at work on the sequel.

Kristi Hemingway-Weatherall ("The First Thing about Love") is a writer, performing artist, and English/theater teacher. Her greatest role to date is as Mom to Levi and Eden. While living in Denver, Colorado, she often dreams of Southern France. You can find Kristi's writing in countless magazines and anthologies. She has just completed her first novel.

Erika Hoffman ("Intestinal Fortitude") is a narrative essayist whose work has been featured in nationally known magazines and anthologies, including several *Cup of Comfort®* editions. Erika and her husband make their home in North Carolina.

Gina Farella Howley ("180 Seconds to a Lifetime") taught special education for fifteen years. Currently, she is privileged to be a stay-at-home mom to sons Martin, Joseph, and Timothy, in their Naperville, Illinois, home, and to pursue her lifelong dream of writing. She and her husband, John, remain South Siders at heart.

Michelle Hozey ("Love Shack") is a freelance writer and proud Air Force wife. Her work has been published in newspapers, magazines, and online. She and her husband live in Fort Dix, New Jersey, with their superhero cats, Batman and Robin.

Amy Hudock, PhD ("Garlic Soup") is a writer, professor, and editor who lives in South Carolina with her family. She is a co-founder of the e-zine *LiteraryMama* and co-editor of *Literary Mama: Reading for the Maternally Inclined* and *American Women Prose Writers, 1820–1870*. Her essays appear in several *Cup of Comfort*® books; *Ask Me about My Divorce*; *Mama, PhD*; *Single State of the Union*; *Mothering a Movement*; and other anthologies.

Carolyn Huhn-Sullivan ("Heart and Sole") lives in Beaverton, Oregon, with her husband, Dan, and their three children, Jonathan, Nicholas, and Emma. By day she is an executive manager; by night she is a mother, wife, and friend. Carolyn is the oldest grandchild of Arthur and Parina Rodondi; she will be forever grateful to them for their sage marital advice.

Craig Idlebrook ("Retiring Bill Pullman") is a freelance writer in Maine. He's written about parenthood for *Mothering*, *Funny Times*, *Boot Camp for New Dads*, and *A Cup of Comfort*® *for Fathers*. As a reporter and essayist, he is a regular contributor to *Mother Earth News*, *the Hill Country Observer*, and *AAA Northern New England Experience*.

Phyllis Jardine ("First Love") is a retired nurse and military wife living in the Annapolis Valley of Nova Scotia with her husband, Bud, and black Lab, Morgan.

Madeleine M. Kuderick ("Three Little Words") lives on Florida's Gulf Coast with her husband and two children. She works in the fast-paced medical device industry but takes time to enjoy life's simple pleasures, including evening walks with her husband and writing. Her work appears in several other anthologies.

Cathi LaMarche ("Wildly in Love") is the author of the novel *While the Daffodils Danced*. She has written for several anthologies, including *A Cup of Comfort® for Divorced Women* and *A Cup of Comfort® for Dog Lovers II*. She teaches English and writing in Missouri, where she resides with her adventurous husband, two children, and three dogs.

Beverly Lessard ("Who Could Ask for Anything More?") and her imperfect husband, Philip, reside in Stow, Massachusetts, where she writes a weekly column for the local newspaper. They have three daughters and eight grandchildren. Beverly received an engineering degree from the University of Maine in 1972, and in 1986 she started Boxboro Children's Center.

Tina Lincer ("When His and Hers Becomes Ours") has written for numerous newspapers, magazines, and anthologies; her personal essays also have aired on public radio. A former labor editor and dance critic, she lives in upstate New York, where she is associate director of communications at Union College. She is at work on a novel and a memoir.

Patricia Ljutic ("Love Check"), a registered nurse, lives in California with her husband, son, a variety of art projects, a dog, and two rats. Her work has appeared in regional and national publications, including *A Cup of Comfort®for Parents of Children with Special Needs* and *My Mom Is My Hero*.

Allison Maher ("Girlfriend") lives on a small fruit farm in Aylesford, Nova Scotia, with her boyfriend, Dave. She is a full-time farmer and part-time writer. Her first novel, *I, The Spy*, was nominated for the Red Cedar Readers' Choice Award and has been listed on *Kayak Magazine's* Recommended Reading List. *Cup of Comfort®* editor Colleen Sell is her favorite elf.

Tina Wagner Mattern ("My Other Husband") is a Portland, Oregon, hairstylist and writer who has been published several times in internationally known short-story anthologies. She has been happily married for thirty years to Fred/ Freddie and is the mother of a twenty-nine-year-old son, Aaron, and a twenty-six-year-old daughter, Summer.

Lorri McDole ("Biscuits and Olives") has published stories in various print and online publications, including *Brain/Child*, *The Rambler*, *Eclectica*, *A Cup of Comfort*® *for Writers*, *Epiphany*, and *New Madrid*. She was a finalist in the 2007 Annie Dillard Creative Nonfiction Contest (*Bellingham Review*) and lives in a Seattle suburb with her husband and two children.

Jann Mitchell-Sandstrom ("A Love Worth Waiting For") is a retired journalist and the author of four books. She lives in Oregon, Sweden, and Tanzania—always with her hand out for donations for the Bibi Jann Children's Care Trust (*www.bibijann.org*). From African fabrics, she quilts ethnic wall-hangings to sell on behalf of her *bibis*. She urges others to always follow their hearts.

Wade Morgan ("Lost and Found"), a native of Seward, Alaska, spent his youth enjoying the simple pleasures of childhood in rural Alaska. He finally grew up at the age of forty-three, and shortly thereafter met the love of his life, Martha. He writes for the pleasure it brings to him and to others who may enjoy his stories.

Faith Paulsen ("Love Imitates Art") has published her writing in *A Cup of Comfort*® *for Parents of Children with Special Needs* and *A Cup of Comfort*® *for Mothers* as well as *Literary Mama* and *Wild River Review*. She lives in suburban Philadelphia with her husband, Bart, three kids, and various pets.

Mary C. M. Phillips ("Love and the Un-Romantic") is a musician and writer of poetry and short stories. She has toured nationally as a keyboardist, bass player, and singer for various rock groups and musical comedy artists. She resides in New York with her husband and son.

Felice Prager ("The Almost-Proposal") is a freelance writer and multisensory educational therapist from Scottsdale, Arizona. Hundreds of her essays have been published locally, nationally, and internationally in print and on the Internet. She is the author of *Quiz It: Arizona*.

Julie Clark Robinson ("The Piece of Paper That Almost Blinded Me") is (still) married to David—happily, in fact. While list-making remains part of her life, she restricts the contents to freelance writing projects. She is the author of *Live in the Moment*, and her essays have appeared in *Family Circle* and several *Cup of Comfort*® anthologies.

Deborah Shouse ("How the Funny Papers Rocked My World") is a writer, speaker, editor, and creativity catalyst. Her writing has appeared in *The Washington Post*, *Reader's Digest*, *Newsweek*, *Woman's Day*, *Family Circle*, *Spirituality & Health*, and *The Chicago Tribune*. She has authored a variety of books and writes a weekly love story column for the *Kansas City Star*.

Stephanie Springsteen ("The Prism") is a former software developer and now a full-time mom living in Chicago with her husband and two children. She wrote for Loyola University's literary journal, *Cadence*, as an undergraduate and has been studying memoir for the past three years at StoryStudio Chicago.

Joyce Stark ("A Gift for Women") lives in northeast Scotland. She travels widely in the United States and Europe and writes travel articles as well as essays for U.S. and European publications, including several *Cup of Comfort®* books.

Sylvia Suriano-Diodati ("Love, Italian Style") is a piano teacher, songwriter, and writer of short stories and poetry. She lives in the outskirts of Toronto with her husband, Ludovico, and their daughter, Isabella. A hopeless romantic, Sylvia is currently working on a novel series, hoping to inspire young readers with her passion for love, life, and spirituality.

Barbara Neal Varma ("Dancing with My Husband") is an award-winning writer in Southern California who has written for *Image*, *Toastmaster Magazine*, *WritersWeekly. com*, and various other magazines and literary journals. Her essays have won awards from *Writer's Digest*, the National Writers Association, and *Anthology* magazine.

Samantha Ducloux Waltz ("Supersized Love") is an award-winning freelance writer in Portland, Oregon. Her stories can be seen in the *Cup of Comfort®* series and numerous other anthologies. Ray, her husband, is often her muse. Samantha has also published fiction and nonfiction under the name Samellyn Wood.

Kelly Wilson ("The Anniversary Gift") is a busy mom and freelance writer. She is the author of *Live Cheap & Free! Strategies to Thrive in Tough Economic Times* as well as numerous articles and short stories for children and adults. Kelly lives with her husband and two small children in Portland, Oregon.

Mary E. Winter ("Built with Tender Loving Care") is a retired teacher who is currently writing a mystery/romance novel. She and her carpenter husband live in rural Wisconsin. They recently built a playhouse for their three granddaughters, who love to sleep out there and make up their own stories.

Suzanne Yoder ("Willow Weep No More") is an elementary school teacher who lives in Kalona, Iowa, with her husband and two children, Jackson and Alison. This is the first story she has written specifically for publication; she felt her parents' story was too remarkable not to be shared. After five months in the rehabilitation center, her dad returned home, where he continues his rehabilitation with his bride by his side.

Debra Gordon Zaslow ("Diving for Love") lives in Ashland, Oregon, with her husband, a rabbi. She has an MFA in writing and teaches both storytelling at Southern Oregon University and memoir writing courses in the community. Her CD, *Return Again*, features Jewish stories of healing and transformation. She has recently completed a memoir, *Bringing Bubbe Home*, about caring for her 103-year-old grandmother.

About the Author

Colleen Sell has compiled and edited thirty-five volumes of the *Cup of Comfort*® book series. She has authored, ghostwritten, or edited more than one hundred books. A seasoned journalist, she's also been editor-in-chief of two award-winning consumer magazines, a newspaper columnist, a features writer, and an associate editor of a business magazine. She and her husband, T.N. Trudeau, live in an ancient farmhouse on a forty-acre pioneer homestead in the Pacific Northwest, where they share an abiding love of family, nature, dancing, and one another.

COME SEE WHAT'S BREWING AT
CUP OF COMFORT.COM

Be inspired. Be uplifted. Be involved.

www.cupofcomfort.com

With our enhanced, community-focused website, readers can:

- Share their thoughts, experiences, ideas, and more in our community forums

- Submit stories for possible inclusion in future volumes

- Receive professional editorial feedback through the Critique Program

- Participate in our informative writing webinars

- Subscribe to our *Cup of Comfort*® newsletter

- Enjoy featured stories

- And more!